Arturo Azurdia believes that much modern preaching is powerless. Sadly, he is right. He is also convinced that the reason for this tragic truth is an absence of the unction that only the Holy Spirit can bring, and in a searching and warm-hearted analysis he shows how the situation should and can be remedied.

Were this book to be read, absorbed and acted upon by all involved in the preaching – and hearing – of the Word of God there would be a revolution in the Christian church. I wholeheartedly commend this splendid publication.

John Blanchard

On one memorable afternoon, while having tea in Ealing with Dr. Martyn Lloyd-Jones, I seized the opportunity to ask the Doctor a question: 'Isn't it difficult at times to tell whether one is preaching in the energy of the flesh or the power of the Spirit?'

'Not at all,' he replied. 'When you preach in the energy of the flesh, you feel exalted and lifted up. When you preach in the power of the Spirit, you are filled with humble awe at the work of God.'

Not many days later, at a student conference in Schloss Mittersill, an Inter-Varsity center in Austria, the Lord gave me that humbling realization as he chose to bless a late afternoon message with his power.

This heart-searching book by Arturo Azurdia III has convicted me again of the work of the Spirit as the *sine qua non* of fruit in preaching. The author writes as a pastor to preachers, declaring that the preached word will transform lives only as the Spirit uses it. He shows us ourselves, possessed by a holy compulsion, but given an impossible task. We cannot give life to the spiritually dead. Knowing our own weakness and foolishness, and the weakness and foolishness of those whom God will call, we preach a message that is foolishness to men but the power of God to salvation.

Prayer for the filling of the Spirit is therefore as necessary as the labor of workmen in the Word. Prayer cannot command the Spirit, nor can we always tell when or how the Spirit uses his Word. But we are shown Charles Haddon Spurgeon climbing the fifteen steps to the platform of the Metropolitan Tabernacle repeating, 'I believe in the Holy Ghost!'

If prayer for the Spirit's unction is a pillar of your ministry, you will be delighted with this book. It deals clearly with Scriptural teaching, quotes lavishly from the Puritans and contemporary sources, and reminds you that, because the Spirit always witnesses to Christ, you must do so, too. If your praying for the Spirit's power has become formal or thoughtless then this book can change both you and your ministry – by the Spirit's power.

Edmund P. Clowney

Seldom does a book arise of which one can say, 'This should be essential reading for preachers at whatever stage of their ministry!' But I can say this honestly of this book. I have found it compelling reading because of its timeliness, its helpful insights, its encouragements and warnings. The best commendation I can give is that it overwhelmed me with the privilege of proclaiming the unsearchable riches of the Lord Jesus. It has filled me afresh with an awareness of my dependence upon the Holy Spirit and a desire for His empowerment. It has made me wish that I could start all over again.

Derek Prime

Many talk about the necessity of unction but few understand what unction is. Having unction is like being in love. You know when you have it but you have difficulty defining it. Arturo Azurdia, in his well written book, *Spirit Empowered Preaching*, not only defines unction but also gives an exegetical defence for expecting and seeking the role of the Holy Spirit in your preaching. When you finish reading this book, not only will you have a better idea of the role of the Spirit in preaching, but you will also know better how to preach in dependence on the Holy Spirit. Everyone who is preaching or preparing to preach needs to read this book.

Joseph A. Pipa, Jr.
President,
Greenville Presbyterian Theological Seminary
Greenville, South Carolina

SPIRIT EMPOWERED PREACHING

Involving The Holy Spirit in Your Ministry

ARTURO G. AZURDIA III

Mentor

Christian Focus Publications
publishes books for all ages

Our mission statement -

STAYING FAITHFUL

In dependence upon God we seek to help make His infallible word, the Bible, relevant. Our aim is to ensure that the Lord Jesus Christ is presented as the only hope to obtain forgiveness of sin, live a useful life and look forward to heaven with Him.

REACHING OUT

Christ's last command requires us to reach out to our world with His gospel. We seek to help fulfill that by publishing books that point people towards Jesus and help them to develop a Christ-like maturity. We aim to equip all levels of readers for life, work, ministry and mission.

Books in our adult range are published in three imprints.

Christian Focus contains popular works including biographies, commentaries, basic doctrine, and Christian living. Our children's books are also published in this imprint.

Mentor focuses on books written at a level suitable for Bible College and seminary students, pastors, and other serious readers. The imprint includes commentaries, doctrinal studies, examination of current issues, and church history.

Christian Heritage contains classic writings from the past.

© Arturo G. Azurdia III

ISBN 1857924134

Scripture quotations are from the New American Standard Bible,
© copyright The Lockman Foundation,
1960, 1962, 1963, 1968, 1971, 1972, 1973, 1975, 1977

Published in 1998, reprinted in 2003 in the Mentor imprint
by Christian Focus Publications
Geanies House, Fearn, Ross-shire, IV20 1TW, Great Britain

www.christianfocus.com

Cover design by Alister MacInnes

Printed and bound in Scotland by
Bell & Bain, Glasgow

Contents

Foreword by *John H. Armstrong* 9

Introduction 11

1. The Greater Works 17

2. The Sacred Communicator 29

3. The Christocentric Spirit 48

4. The Evangelical Priority 66

5. The Decisive Function of the Church 80

6. The *Sine Qua Non* of Gospel Preaching...................... 97

7. The Occupational Vulnerability of Preaching............... 116

8. Preaching and the Man of God 131

9. The Sensitive Spirit... 149

10. Pray Me Full 164

Summary.. 178

Bibliography 184

Indices 188

DEDICATION

To Lori, my beloved wife,

and to Katherine and Jonathan, gracious gifts of God

May God use us all
for the greater glory of Jesus Christ

ACKNOWLEDGEMENTS

It has been said, 'An expert is a person who has read a great deal in a particular field of study. A scholar is a person who has read everything in a particular field of study.'

By these definitions I am certainly no scholar. For that matter, neither am I an expert. I am, without shame, a local church pastor of average gifts. My life, however, has been steadily improved by people used of God to benefit me in unimaginable ways.

The realization of this fact has become all the more poignant to me throughout this project. To the following I would like to express my deepest appreciation and affection:

To Arturo and Joy Azurdia, my father and mother, who have been the foremost instruments of God's gracious providence in my life.

To Frank Griffith, my dear friend, whose Spirit empowered preaching wonderfully benefitted the saints at Christ Community Church during my sabbatical.

To Steve Fernandez, a true Barnabas, whose faithful encouragement has been a gift from God during some of the darkest moments in my ministry.

To Dr. John Armstrong, who through his own ministry of proclamation first opened my eyes to Spirit empowered preaching. He is both an authentic Christian and a true reformer, an exceedingly rare combination.

To Reverend Thomas N. Smith, a man who models everything this project seeks to set forth. He is the finest preacher of the Christian religion I know.

To the faculty at Westminster Seminary in Escondido, particularly Dr. Joseph Pipa (now president of Greenville Theological Seminary), who powerfully reinforced my commitment to the theology of preaching, and Dr. Edmund Clowney, whose influence not only effected my preaching but altered my Christian life. He convinced me that the Scriptures are to be read Christocentrically.

8

SPIRIT EMPOWERED PREACHING

To Al Ekin, Dave Valdix, Mike Rohrer, Kevin Shea, Don Doehla, and Kevin Jackson, the elders and deacons of Christ Community Church. Never has a pastor been blessed by such fine partners and loyal brothers.

To the faithful men in the Saturday morning prayer group. They 'pray me full' each week.

To the beloved saints at Christ Community Church. How I long to preach for you in the power of the Spirit of God.

To Constance Johnston, a theological musician, who has embraced the truths of this book and beautified them with her gift.

Foreword

The work of preaching absorbs the interest and passion of God-called men virtually every waking moment of every day. Sometimes it even awakens us in the night with an ever deepening realization of the humbling question, 'Who is sufficient for these things?' Martyn Lloyd-Jones once said, 'To me the work of preaching is the highest and greatest and the most glorious calling to which anyone can ever be called.' How could any God-called herald not agree? And yet how can any who preaches regularly not be deeply aware of how infrequently he knows 'the sweet piercing of the Spirit' by the preached Word into the hearts of his people?

Preaching, in our time, has clearly undergone significant change. Often the preacher, even the evangelical preacher, is not more than a dispenser of new data (biblical or otherwise), or a motivator and spiritual counselor for spiritually starved and confused people. What is most obviously missing is 'the burden'. There is no 'woe' to be felt in the preacher's tone or spirit. And where there is no true burden, or woe, there is no true or lasting blessing!

What is needed in the West, now more than ever, is biblical reformation and God-sent revival. Art Azurdia's excellent book, *Spirit Empowered Preaching*, profoundly addresses the need for reformation and revival in the pulpit. He takes the teachable reader through the important biblical texts, always pointing him to 'preaching Christ and him crucified' as the true theme of the whole Bible. He shows what is needed to accomplish this work and he warmly urges us to get power from God as well as material to deliver.

I can't begin to number the times I have heard sermons and said to myself, 'What my brother says is true but so what?' Or, 'Does this man really believe his message?'

Art Azurdia will convince you, if your mind and heart is open to God, to get power as well as material. He will not disdain the hard work of study, especially of exegesis, but he will convince you that having done all of this work you must still deal with God for grace and power in the Spirit. If your people would hear God, not just you the preacher, you must bring more to the act of preaching than orthodoxy.

What has 'unction' or 'anointing' to do with preaching? How are we to 'ask the Father for the Spirit'\(Luke 11:13) in terms of preaching? Is there an access of Holy Spirit power that truly falls upon the preacher and hearer which demonstrates, beyond question, that God is speaking and his people know it? Art Azurdia believes that there most certainly is and will show you why, with Scriptural argumentation. If he is right, and I believe he is, then this could be one of the most important books to come along in many years for the reformation of the church in our time.

I pray this fine book will have an ever increasing effect upon those called to preach. My prayer is that God will give it a wide audience and life changing fruitfulness for years to come. I intend to read it again and again and to widely recommend it to pastors the world over.

John H. Armstrong
President,
Reformation and Revival Ministries

INTRODUCTION

Careful, meditative, and painstaking exegesis must be the foundation for an expository ministry. All doctrine and theology with its attendant application must be the result of a literal, grammatical, historical, contextual, redemptive comprehension of the sacred text. Any attempt at preaching apart from this *a priori* commitment is to undercut the very substance of proclamation.

Having affirmed this, however, we must also acknowledge the potential liability to which we who approach Holy Writ in this fashion are particularly susceptible. Consider the insight of one prominent British preacher:

> One of the great perils that face preachers ... is the problem of hyper-intellectualism, that is, the constant danger of lapsing into a purely cerebral form of proclamation, which falls exclusively upon the intellect. Men become obsessed with doctrine and end up as brain-oriented preachers. There is consequently a fearful impoverishment in their hearers emotionally, devotionally, and practically. Such pastors are men of books and not men of people; they know the doctrines, but they know nothing of the emotional side of religion. They set little store upon experience or upon constant fellowship and interaction with almighty God. It is one thing to explain the truth of Christianity to men and women; it is another thing to feel the overwhelming power of the sheer loveliness and enthrallment of Jesus Christ and to communicate that dynamically to the whole person who listens so that there is a change of such dimensions that he loves Him with all his heart and soul and mind and strength.[1]

What kind of preaching is it that causes men and women 'to feel the overwhelming power of the sheer loveliness and enthrallment of Jesus Christ' ... that compels a person to love the Lord Jesus 'with all his heart and soul and mind and strength?' It is preaching that emerges from diligent exegesis, to be sure. But more than that, it is preaching that is infused with a power, *a vitality*, that infinitely exceeds the scope of human strength. It is a vitality that can only be attributed to the divine; a vitality that originates from heaven itself.

It is my deep conviction that the greatest deficiency in contemporary expositional ministry is powerlessness; in other words, preaching that is devoid of the vitality of the Holy Spirit. The Puritans of old referred to it simply as 'that certain unction'. Others have spoken of it as 'the anointing'. Whether or not these terms most appropriately reflect the biblical theology of Spirit-empowered preaching is not of concern at this moment. That they capture the *sine qua non* of authentic preaching as revealed in the biblical record is undeniable.

Stated more explicitly, it is

> ... the Holy Spirit falling upon the preacher in a special manner. It is an access of power. It is God giving power, an enabling, through the Spirit, to the preacher in order that he may do this work in a manner that lifts it up beyond the efforts and endeavours of man to a position in which the preacher is being used by the Spirit and becomes the channel through whom the Spirit works.[2]

Allow me to ask you, fellow preacher: do you deeply desire this experience when you ascend into the pulpit? Do you beseech heaven to dispatch a Spirit-vitalized word when you stand before the people of God? Sadly, it would appear that for a great many today this is a dimension of preaching that is altogether ignored. Though studies on the subject of preaching proliferate, right techniques are promoted as the guarantee of effectiveness while dependence upon the Holy Spirit is given token consideration, if mentioned at all. A cursory view of contemporary homiletic literature quickly establishes this analysis.

To be sure, certain techniques are essential to effective preaching, particularly the exegetical techniques needed to discern the Spirit-intended meaning of a preaching portion. However, apart from the quickening power of the Holy Spirit in the act of proclamation, even the best and most essential technique falls miserably short of transforming those to whom we preach. J. I. Packer writes:

> The churches of the West are currently in confusion about the way to make preaching spiritually significant for the modern congregation, and are treating the problem as primarily one of devising appropriate techniques. Technique is, of course, necessary in preaching .... But the Puritans themselves would be the first to insist that there is more to significant preaching than mere technique, even applicatory technique.[3]

Packer then concludes by quoting Richard Baxter: 'All our work must be done spiritually, as men possessed of the Holy Ghost.'[4]

In a nutshell, here is the thesis for which I am contending: the efficacious empowerment of the Spirit of God is indispensable to the ministry of proclamation. But surely this must be followed by an obvious question. If this thesis is biblically justifiable why then is the ignorance, or even worse, the disregard of the ministry of the Spirit in relationship to preaching so widespread in our time?

Many compelling answers could be offered. Nevertheless, one appears to be preeminent above all others. The neglect of the ministry of the Spirit in the work of preaching has emerged as a result of a failure to see the full-orbed implications of the nature of sinful humanity. Stated more directly, one's understanding of human depravity will determine the extent to which dependence is placed upon the sovereign Spirit of God.

Consider for a moment the biblical record regarding the nature of man: 'The heart is more deceitful than all else and is desperately sick; who can understand it?' (Jer. 17:9). Paul states that unbelievers walk 'in the futility of their mind, being darkened in their understanding, excluded from the life of God, because of the ignorance that is in them, because of the hardness of their heart' (Eph. 4:17-18). The unregenerate are by definition 'dead in trespasses and sins' (Eph. 2:1), possessing hearts that have been blinded by 'the god of this world' (2 Cor. 4:4).

No human eloquence or rhetoric can convince men dead in sin of the truth of God. The unquickened heart is impenetrable. Spurgeon says:

> I shall not attempt to teach a tiger the virtues of vegetarianism; but I shall as hopefully attempt that task as I would try to convince an unregenerate man of the truths revealed by God concerning sin, and righteousness, and judgment to come. These spiritual truths are repugnant to carnal men, and the carnal mind cannot receive the things of God. Gospel truth is diametrically opposed to fallen nature; and if I have not a power much stronger than that which lies in moral suasion, or in my own explanations and arguments, I have undertaken a task in which I am sure of defeat . . . Except the Lord endow us with power from on high, our labour must be in vain, and our hopes must end in disappointment.[5]

Simply stated, to attempt a preaching ministry apart from an active dependence upon the vitality of the Spirit of God is to blatantly disregard our biblical anthropology. We affirm that the opening of the heart is a divine prerogative (Luke 24:45), the monergistic work of God (Acts 16:14). The most gifted preacher is impotent to inaugurate a saving experience apart from a gracious work of the omnipotent Spirit. Therefore, any effective ministry of exposition must include both a resolute commitment to the practice of diligent exegesis and a thoroughgoing dependence upon the ministry of the Holy Spirit.

Now we must ask, 'Do the scriptures speak specifically to this issue of vitality in preaching?' Absolutely. There exists within the pages of biblical revelation a definitive theology of Spirit-empowered preaching, as we will discover. For the moment, however, I urge you to reflect upon the commission of the original preachers of the gospel:

> 'Thus it is written, that the Christ should suffer and rise again from the dead the third day; and that repentance for forgiveness of sins should be proclaimed in His name to all the nations, beginning from Jerusalem. You are witnesses of these things' (Luke 24:46-48).

Consider these men. They were afforded the finest preparation for ministry ever experienced. They had communed with God incarnate for three years, benefiting from His constant instruction and observing innumerable displays of seemingly limitless power. Three of them were firsthand witnesses of His manifest glory at the Mount of Transfiguration. All of them had observed His crucifixion, and most importantly, His power over death in resurrection. If ever a man had been equipped for preaching the gospel, these men were. No theological institution could ever hope to duplicate the privileges granted them. Yet the omniscient Christ knew that if left to themselves these privileged men would meet with nothing but failure and antagonism. Therefore, to meet the demands of a commission impossible to accomplish in human strength, He promised a source of power that would infinitely transcend human potency:

'And behold, I am sending forth the promise of My Father upon you; but you are to stay in the city until you are clothed with power from on high' (Luke 24:49).

Luke later records:

'... but you shall receive power when the Holy Spirit has come upon you; and you shall be My witnesses both in Jerusalem, and in all Judea and Samaria, and even to the remotest part of the earth' (Acts 1:8).

Of course, the unfolding of the book of Acts reveals the fulfilment of this promise, perhaps most graphically displayed on the Day of Pentecost when a Spirit-empowered Peter preached a simple exposition of a few Old Testament texts. What occurred? Truth was united with fire and consequently three thousand people were added to the Kingdom of God.

Twenty centuries later, the baton of the Great Commission has been handed to us. The circumstances we face are almost identical to those of the disciples. The message is the same. The nature of unconverted man is as it has always been. Perhaps the only substantial difference is that we are not the men the disciples were. For all of our educational opportunities, we have not been given the inestimable privilege of learning directly from Jesus. The conclusion, then, is obvious: if they were men in need of the vitality of the Spirit for the proclamation of the gospel, we, at the very least, are equally needy. It is, at last, the epitome of foolishness to attempt to carry out the exposition of the gospel devoid of the vitality of God the Spirit.

A Presbyterian minister of a previous generation made this penetrating statement with which I conclude:

> The great want of today is a holier ministry. We do not need more stalwart polemics, more mighty apologists, or preachers who compass a wide range of natural knowledge, important though these be. But we need men of God who bring the atmosphere of heaven with them to the pulpit and speak from the borders of another world.[6]

Notes

1. Geoffrey Thomas, 'Powerful Preaching', *The Preacher and Preaching,* ed. Samuel Logan, Jr. (Phillipsburg: Presbyterian and Reformed Publishing Company, 1986), p. 369.

2. D. Martyn Lloyd-Jones, *Preaching & Preachers* (Grand Rapids: Zondervan Publishing House, 1971), p. 305.

3. J. I. Packer, *A Quest for Godliness* (Wheaton: Crossway Books, 1990), p. 289.

4. Richard Baxter, *The Reformed Pastor* (repr. ed., Carlisle: The Banner of Truth Trust, 1989), p. 120.

5. Charles Spurgeon, *An All-Round Ministry* (repr. ed., Carlisle: The Banner of Truth Trust, 1986), p. 322.

6. This is an anonymous quote read by Iain Murray in a tape-recorded sermon entitled 'The Problems of Contemporary Evangelism'.

1

THE GREATER WORKS

It is not only Catholic Christendom which has been guilty of seeking
to domesticate the Holy Spirit.... Protestants have been no less
anxious to do so, for the Holy Spirit is a disturbing influence.
MICHAEL GREEN

If Pentecost is not repeated, neither is it retracted ...
This is the era of the Holy Spirit
JOHN MURRAY

The best man here, if he knows what he is,
knows that he is out of his depth in his sacred calling.
CHARLES HADDON SPURGEON

The Question That Forces The Issue

At the crack of dawn on an Easter Sunday morning eleven years
ago, April 19, 1987, I hopped out of bed brimming with the
excitement of an anxious child on Christmas morning. The fact
is, I had slept very little the night before, but my adrenalin was in
overdrive. Everything about which I had thought and prayed for
the previous several months had led me to this moment: the first
public worship service of North Bay Bible Church.[1]

One of the most vivid memories of that morning came when I
found an unexpected greeting card sitting on our kitchen table.
Since it had been addressed to me I opened the envelope and
pulled out an Easter card embossed with a typical Easter greeting.
Underneath the printed greeting, however, were these handwritten
words from my wife:

No matter what happens, these are exciting days. I will never regret
coming to Vallejo, and no one is prouder of you than me.

I love you,

Lori.

Do you hear the sense of the unexpected in those words ... *no
matter what happens*? Now, we were not altogether naive.
Common sense told us that we ought to anticipate a few surprises.
But the fact remained, we had never before planted a church.
Certainly we had no idea then that ten years later we would find
ourselves looking back over a decade of ministry, having
concluded that our experience had been altogether different from
anything we had anticipated. On the one hand, had we possessed
a foreknowledge of the providential challenges we would face
as a congregation it is highly unlikely we would have attempted
to plant this church. Far surpassing these unexpected challenges,
however, were the unanticipated depths of joy we would come
to know as a result of observing the manifestations of the grace
of God in the lives of people. Through my pastoral journey I
have come to realize that God's sweet and bitter providences,
unexpected though they may be, are always an expression of His
perfection.

Consequently, such a realization has served to accomplish
two purposes in my life. First of all, it has filled me with an
enthusiasm to press ahead into the next ten years. To be sure, the
past must not be forgotten. The lessons learned from ministerial
failures must not be ignored, nor the manifold dispensations of
God's undeserved goodness. But we must not live in the past.
Instead, if we are to be good stewards of the grace that God has
bestowed upon us in past days of ministry, then it is incumbent
upon us to seek for the greater glory of His Son in both the present
and the future. Eleven years of ministry has not jaded me. It has
intensified my appetite for greater fruitfulness.

But this past decade of ministry has served a second purpose
as well. Not only has it deepened my desire to see greater
manifestations of the grace of God, it has simultaneously served

to school me in the subject of my own inabilities. Pastoral ministry is exceedingly effective in making a man more acutely aware of his manifold inadequacies. And so, as a man called of God to gospel ministry, I find myself stuck between the proverbial rock and hard place; living with the uneasy tension that grows out of an insatiable desire for greater fruitfulness, and, the simultaneous recognition of the utter inability to realize that desire in my own strength.

That haunting dilemma, common to every preacher of the gospel, drives us to seek an answer to the following question: *by what means will we who are powerless accomplish the work that God Himself has burdened us to do?*

In part, this is the question that the disciples of Jesus Christ were asking themselves on the night before His death.

A Historical Parallel

Just prior to His arrest in the Garden of Gethsemane, Jesus spent an evening with His disciples that they would never forget. It was on that evening that Jesus girded Himself with a towel and stooped to wash the feet of these men. It was on that evening that Jesus exposed the apparently trustworthy Judas Iscariot as the betrayer to the rest of the unsuspecting disciples. It was on that evening that Jesus instituted the sacred supper. Alone, each of these events were of great significance. To experience them collectively within a brief span of time was undoubtedly overwhelming.

The most pressing concern to the disciples, however, was the announcement of Jesus regarding His imminent departure (John 13:33). Moreover, His emphatic declaration that they could not go away with Him precipitated an emotional crisis on their part. Living in the wake of the resurrection, contemporary Christians have the distinct advantage of knowing that His going away was for the purpose of effecting the work of redemption. The disciples, however, had no such advantage. To be sure, Jesus had spoken openly with them concerning His death and resurrection, but they had steadily failed to grasp the implications of His words (cf.

Luke 18:31-33). Consequently, when the reality of His departure became evident, they were thrown into great emotional travail.

It is for this reason that Jesus then turns His attention toward comforting these men in John 14. For example, though His going away is a return to the Father's house, He assures them that it is a house with sufficient room for each of them (John 14:2). In fact, He informs them that the reason for His going away is to prepare a place for them in this house, and that in due time He Himself will personally return for them (John 14:3). Moreover, they need not fear their inability to know the way to His Father's house. They know Him, and He is the way (John 14:4-6). Given ample time for consideration all of this would prove to supply significant comfort for these grieving men.

A critical question still lingers in the minds of the disciples, however. 'What about the intervening time between the departure of Jesus and His return?' After all, sometime earlier Jesus had called these men to ministry. In fact, He had called them to be preachers of the gospel (cf. Matt. 10:7; Mark 3:14). By all accounts they took this call seriously. Whether fishing nets or tax tables, they had surrendered everything to do this work. They undoubtedly assumed it to be a lifelong endeavor. Were they mistaken? Certainly at this point, with the departure of Jesus at hand, was it not safe to assume that a change had occurred in the original design? But no change can be detected in the words of Jesus. In fact, as His discourse continues in John 14, it becomes apparent to the disciples that His purpose for their future ministry has in no way deviated from its original intent: 'Truly, truly I say to you, he who believes in Me, the works that I do shall he do also; and greater works than these shall he do ...' (John 14:12).

To be sure, these men were devastated by the thought of His departure. Even more to the point, to give even slight consideration to the continuance of this gospel ministry in His absence seemed beyond rational comprehension. After all, from firsthand experience they had observed the kind of vehement opposition Jesus had aroused. Though a few people were responsive to His message, most had reacted with hostility and antagonism. Several attempts had already been made against His life. While it was easy to be courageous in His presence, the thought of continuing His work apart from Him seemed suicidal. Moreover, present in their consciousness was the painful awareness of their repeated failures: the fear of Peter when Jesus commanded Him to walk on the Sea of Galilee (Matt. 14:25-31), the faithlessness of Philip when Jesus sought to feed the five thousand (John 6:5-7), the hard-heartedness of James and John who wished to call fire down from heaven to consume a village of unbelieving Samaritans (Luke 9:52-55), their collective arrogance as they argued over personal greatness and supremacy (Mark 9:33-37). But more apparent than all previous shortcomings was the fresh sting of their failure earlier that same evening as they became the recipients of an act of lowly and humble service on the part of Jesus Himself, who bowed to do for them what they had refused to do for Him. The reality of yet another failure was painfully impressed upon them with every touch of His hands on their dirty feet.

Of course, without hesitation it can be said that these men dearly loved the Lord Jesus Christ. They had given up everything to follow Him. Despite their deeply-rooted carnalities, they longed for people to acknowledge Him as Messiah. Yet weakness and inadequacy continually expressed themselves in their lives. It would be no surprise, then, were we to discover that they were asking of themselves something akin to the question asked earlier: *By what means will we who are powerless accomplish the work that Jesus Himself has burdened us to do?*

They had learned a painful lesson throughout the previous several months; namely, that when left to themselves, failure was the inevitable consequence. It is at this very point, however, in the shadow of His departure, that Jesus now speaks His most comforting words to these men: left to themselves they would never be.

The Greater Works

Before moving ahead, it is essential to define the phrase 'greater works'.[2] A common interpretation is to define this as a promise to the disciples that they will perform greater miracles than those performed by Jesus. Such an interpretation, however, necessitates the asking of an obvious question: is this particular interpretation borne out by the evidence that appears in the historical record of the book of Acts? Nowhere, for example, do we read of an apostle walking on water. We do not find anything approximating the feeding of multitudes or the transformation of water into wine by means of miraculous intervention. No record is found of any apostolic figure giving sight to the blind, a peculiar manifestation of Messianic credentials.[3] While it is true that Peter prayed on behalf of a woman who was subsequently brought back to life (Acts 9:40), we do not read of an apostle raising someone four days dead and sealed in a tomb. One must keep in mind that to whatever Jesus here refers it must in some sense be 'greater' by comparison than His own experience. Is it accurate to suggest that the apostles were given the ability to perform greater miracles than those of Jesus Himself? Apparently not.

Consider an alternative perspective by the way of two questions. Firstly, how *extensive* was the earthly ministry of Jesus Christ? Not extensive at all by modern standards. The geographical length of first-century Palestine was approximately one hundred and fifty miles, with a width less than half of its length. Secondly, how *influential* was the earthly ministry of Jesus Christ? Not exceedingly influential. It is highly unlikely that the Church Growth people would have included Jesus in their literature when giving consideration to those ministers who have had the greatest breadth of public influence. Here, on the night before His death, He is surrounded by eleven men. Shortly after the resurrection we find that one hundred and twenty are gathered together (Acts 1:15). It is a modest following, to be sure, but in no way could His ministry be considered extensive, nor would anyone reckon it to be wildly influential.

But beginning with the Day of Pentecost a radical change is

set in motion. Peter preaches one sermon and three thousand people are converted. Nothing recorded in the Gospels even remotely resembles this kind of response, whether the earthly ministry of Jesus is considered from the perspective of isolated experiences or taken cumulatively. The 'greater works' to which Jesus here refers are the conversions of people and the advancement of the gospel. In retrospect, they have reference to the spoils of the past twenty centuries of Christian conquest; that is, the ongoing deliverance of people who at one point in time were living among those marked out for eternal judgment. This number of people is so great that, according to the writer of the Apocalypse, it will defy human calculation. It is a vast humanity 'from every nation and all tribes and peoples and tongues' (Rev. 7:9). On the great and final day the fulfillment of the promise of 'the greater works' will be plainly seen; effects that will prove to be both extensive and influential.

The Problem Of Powerlessness
The dilemma of powerlessness has, as yet, remained unaddressed by Jesus. At this point the disciples know only that the accomplishment of 'the greater works' has been promised to them. Again, this begs the previously asked question: *how then will they who are so obviously powerless accomplish the work to which Jesus has appointed them?* Jesus Himself now answers this question: 'Truly, truly I say to you, he who believes in Me, the works that I do shall he do also; and greater works than these shall he do; *because I go to the Father.*'

But what does this phrase mean, 'because I go to the Father'? In the context of Johannine theology it is a reference to the redemptive work of Jesus; *i.e.* His going away via the cross and resurrection.[4] Moreover, later in this discourse Jesus Himself develops the implications of these words:

'But now I am going to Him who sent Me; and none of you asks Me, "Where are You going?" But because I have said these things to you, sorrow has filled your heart. *But I tell you the truth, it is to*

your advantage that I go away; for if I do not go away, the Helper
shall not come to you; but if I go, I will send Him to you. And He,
when He comes, will convict the world concerning sin, and righteousness, and judgment' (John 16:5-8).

This is the fulfillment of the great eschatological promise of the
Old Testament, the promise of a coming day that would inaugurate
a new kind of relationship between God and His people. At the
heart of this new covenant promise were these words: 'And I
will put My Spirit within you' (Ezek. 36:27). And what was it
that purchased these new covenant blessings for the people of
God? The 'going away' of Jesus Christ, all that was involved in
His return to the Father: His death, burial, resurrection, and
ascension. In other words, on the basis of His redemptive
accomplishments Jesus would send the Spirit of God to indwell
His people, thereby furnishing them with the necessary sufficiency
to carry out the greater works. In fact, this is how the Apostle
Peter interprets the 'last days' events of the Day of Pentecost:

'Men of Judea, and all you who live in Jerusalem, let this be known
to you, and give heed to my words. For these men are not drunk, as
you suppose, for it is only the third hour of the day; but this is what
was spoken of through the prophet Joel:

'And it shall be in the last days,
God says,
That I will pour forth of My Spirit upon all mankind ...' (Acts
2:14-17).

But upon what basis could God send His Spirit in this eschatological fulness? Peter answers this question for us:

'Brethren, I may confidently say to you regarding the patriarch
David that he both died and was buried, and his tomb is with us to
this day. And so, because he was a prophet, and knew that God had
sworn to him with an oath to seat one of his descendants upon his
throne, he looked ahead and spoke of the resurrection of the Christ,
that He was neither abandoned to Hades, nor did His flesh suffer

decay. This Jesus God raised up again, to which we are all witnesses. *Therefore having been exalted to the right hand of God, and having received from the Father the promise of the Holy Spirit, He has poured forth this which you both see and hear'* (Acts 2:29-33).

This, we now see, is the justification of Jesus for His departure; so that by the means of His redemptive accomplishments the gift of the indwelling Spirit could be given to His powerless people, consequently supplying them with the adequacy needed to perform the greater works. And in fairness it must be asked, does the book of Acts give any indication that such were the consequences of the advent of the Spirit?

So then, those who had received his word were baptized; and there were added that day about three thousand souls (Acts 2:41).

But many of those who had heard the message believed; and the number of the men came to be about five thousand (Acts 4:4).

And all the more believers in the Lord, multitudes of men and women, were constantly added to their number (Acts 5:14).

Now at this time while the disciples were increasing in number ... (Acts 6:1).

And the word of God kept on spreading; and the number of the disciples continued to increase greatly in Jerusalem, and a great many of the priests were becoming obedient to the faith (Acts 6:7).

So the church throughout all Judea and Galilee and Samaria enjoyed peace, being built up; and, going on in the fear of the Lord and in the comfort of the Holy Spirit, it continued to increase (Acts 9:31).

And all who lived at Lydda and Sharon saw him, and they turned to the Lord (Acts 9:35).

And it became known all over Joppa, and many believed in the Lord (Acts 9:42).

And the hand of the Lord was with them, and a large number who believed turned to the Lord (Acts 11:21).

And considerable numbers were brought to the Lord (Acts 11:24).

But the word of the Lord continued to grow and to be multiplied (Acts 12:24).

And when the Gentiles heard this, they began rejoicing and glorifying the word of the Lord; and as many as had been appointed to eternal life believed. And the word of the Lord was being spread through the whole region (Acts 13:48-49).

And it came about that in Iconium they entered the synagogue of the Jews together, and spoke in such a manner that a great multitude believed, both of Jews and of Greeks (Acts 14:1).

So the churches were being strengthened in the faith, and were increasing in number daily (Acts 16:5).

And some of them were persuaded and joined Paul and Silas, along with a great multitude of the God-fearing Greeks and a number of the leading women (Acts 17:4).

Now these were more noble-minded than those in Thessalonica, for they received the word with great eagerness, examining the scriptures daily, to see whether these things were so. Many of them therefore believed, along with a number of prominent Greek women and men (Acts 17:11-12).

And Crispus, the leader of the synagogue, believed in the Lord with all his household, and many of the Corinthians when they heard were believing and being baptized (Acts 18:8).

So the word of the Lord was growing mightily and prevailing (Acts 19:20).

The in-breaking of the saving reign of Jesus Christ was inaugurated as a consequence of His own soteric achievements; that is to say, the Spirit of the living God came to indwell these disciples and furnish them with the necessary power to accomplish the work that Jesus Christ had burdened their hearts to do.

One final question remains to be asked: *to whom is this promise given?* 'To the original disciples,' some might be quick to suggest. Certainly this promise had direct bearing on the first preachers of the gospel. But consider the words of Jesus carefully: 'Truly, truly I say to you, *he who believes in Me,* the works that I do shall he do also; and greater works than these shall he do; because I go to the Father' (John 14:12). This promise reaches down through the corridors of the centuries and it comes to us at this very present moment. And here, after all, is the answer to our question: *by what means will we who are powerless accomplish the work that God Himself has burdened us to do?*

In the final analysis, we take up our privilege as proclaimers of the gospel, not because we are more intelligent or creative than the world, nor because our powers of rhetorical and logistical techniques are greater than those of other religious spokesmen. None of these powers will ever serve to win one person to Jesus Christ. We must never forget that the Christian Church always advances from a position of human weakness, not human strength (a point we will seek to develop in a later chapter). Instead, we step out to accomplish the greater works because the Spirit of God, on the merits of our Savior's death, has been given to us. According to His own good pleasure He will be pleased to take our feeble and flawed presentations of the gospel and fill them with His irresistible power, consequently overcoming the hearts of sinful people that, otherwise speaking, will prove to be impenetrable.

This is the vitality of the Spirit. Any future in ministry worth having is dependent upon our understanding and embracing of this gift of Jesus Christ to us.

Notes

1. The name of the church was subsequently changed to Christ Community Church.

2. The phrase actually reads 'greater than these will he do', with $\mu\epsilon\iota\zeta ova$, a comparative pronoun followed by the genitive of comparison. The word 'works', $\tau\alpha\ \dot{\epsilon}\rho\gamma\alpha$, is implied from the previous phrase.

3. It is true that Ananias laid hands on Saul of Tarsus and that his temporary blindness consequently disappeared (Acts 9:17-18). But this is hardly the equivalent of the giving of sight as Jesus gave it. See Leon Morris, *The Gospel According to John* (Grand Rapids: William B. Eerdmans Publishing Company, 1971), p. 475.

4. See D. A. Carson, *The Gospel According to John* (Grand Rapids: William B. Eerdmans Publishing Company, 1991), p. 489; and, George R. Beasley-Murray, *John* (Waco: Word Books, Publisher, 1987), p. 255.

2

THE SACRED COMMUNICATOR

God's mind is revealed in the scripture,
but we can see nothing without the spectacles of the Holy Ghost.
THOMAS MANTON

Even the unbeliever encounters God, but he does not penetrate
through to the truth of God that is hidden from him.
KARL BARTH

Apart from the Spirit the Bible is opaque;
with the Spirit it becomes translucent.
DONALD BLOESCH

An Absence Of Truth And Power

I believe that the greatest impediment to the advancement of the gospel in our time is the attempt of the church of Jesus Christ to do the work of God apart from the truth and the power of the Spirit of God. Like the disciples of old, we are powerless, in and of ourselves, to accomplish the 'greater works'. The declaration of Jesus remains true to this day: 'apart from Me you can do nothing' (John 15:5).

At this point, however, powerlessness is not my chief concern. What disturbs me far more deeply is that few contemporary evangelicals seem to be bothered by it. 'What do you mean, powerlessness?' some would question. 'Evangelicalism is bigger than it has ever been before. Consider the size of some of our churches. Take a look at the staggering numbers of some of our men's meetings. People pay attention to us now. Our presence is so powerfully felt that even local and national politicians recognize us as a force with which they must reckon. What do you mean by this "lack of power" talk?' Many evangelicals are altogether oblivious to the real impotence that plagues the Christian community. And why is this the case? Because in these last days of the twentieth century the most popular and significant methods and means for doing ministry require little, if any, divine truth and power.

Consider, for example, the present affair of evangelicalism with secular psychology. By this I do not mean to suggest that there is no place for a ministry of counseling within the Christian church. Nor would I imply that there is nothing whatsoever to be gleaned from the field of psychology. What is of concern to me, however, is that many churches are adopting a paradigm for ministry that is constructed upon and driven by the psychological. For example, pastors are often considered ill-equipped to deal with the deep needs of Christian people unless they have become skilled in the latest psycho-therapeutic techniques. The catalogs of Christian book distributors commonly possess entire sections devoted to advertising the latest books in the field of Christian psychology, including twelve-step study Bibles and twelve-step Bible-study curricula. In various parts of the country local congregations are referring to themselves as twelve-step churches. To be sure, it is not my objective to perform a comprehensive analysis of the Christian counseling movement. Nor is it to call into question the integrity and motivation of Christian counselors. It is to say, however, that even a cursory review of their literature reflects an attempt, whether consciously or unconsciously, to do the work of God apart from the truth and the power of the Spirit of God.

A second way in which the church denies its dependence upon the truth and power of God is seen in the manner in which evangelical denominations have uncritically embraced the techniques of the Church Growth Movement. Ministers are no longer exhorted to pray and fast and preach for conversion. They are challenged to market for it. Most assuredly, certain techniques will gather a crowd of people. Consequently, many have sought to implement them without consideration for the compromise from which the gospel may, and often does, suffer. As a result, when the multitudes do come, many are quick to define their coming as 'revival', when, in reality, they have erroneously confused the presence of physical bodies with the existence of spiritual life. In reality, many of these 'seekers' have not come to flee the wrath of God. They have not come to take up the cross of Jesus Christ. Instead, they have come to add a layer of frosting to their lives. Sadly, they have been promised by the church that such will be the experiential benefits of the Christian religion. A close examination of the results that are being advertised in the name of this movement may reveal the noticeable absence of the fingerprints of the Holy Spirit. This is one of the prevalent ways the church is attempting the work of God apart from the truth and the power of the Spirit of God.

A third way the church reveals its lack of confidence in the truth and power of God is by its commitment to the work of political activism. Again, this is not to suggest that there is no place for a Christian to be politically informed and involved. What is of concern here is the issue of preoccupation and mission. The preoccupation and mission of an evangelical is the evangel. Unfortunately, however, it seems that many have lost their confidence in the power of the gospel to transform. Consequently, time, energy, and financial resources have been redirected toward particular political agendas that, while being conservative, may not even necessarily be Christian. The question, then, must be asked: is this the mandate of the church of Jesus Christ? Is this to be the preoccupation of the people of God, biblically speaking? I think not. Rather, it is a kind of ministry methodology that attempts the work of God apart from the truth and the power of the Spirit of God.

Powerlessness prevails among us. And yet it must be said that this condition is not unique to us. It has been endemic to every moment of evangelical history. What is unique to our time is the extent of our failure to recognize this powerlessness. And why is this the case? In great measure, because the most prominent

methods of ministry in our day do not require the presence of divine
truth and power. They can operate very successfully without them.
Perhaps it is time to give a fresh hearing to the pertinent words of Dr.
Martyn Lloyd-Jones, originally delivered at the annual meeting of
the Inter-Varsity Fellowship in 1954:

> It is being said that the chief need of the Church today is to repent
> because of its 'lack of unity' ... we would suggest that before she
> repents of her disunity, she must repent of her apostasy. She must
> repent of her perversion of, and substitutes for, 'the faith once
> delivered to the saints.' She must repent of setting up her own
> thinking and methods over against the divine revelation in Holy
> Scripture. Here lies the reason for her lack of spiritual power and
> inability to deliver a living message in the power of the Holy Ghost
> to a world ready to perish.[1]

In another place his biographer says similarly:

> He spoke with much force to pastors who, although orthodox in
> their doctrine, were beginning to take up modern evangelistic meth-
> ods in order to promote church growth. The real need, he argued,
> was not for 'campaigns' but for a renewal of the inner life of the
> church and for a restoration of faith in the power of preaching,
> anointed of the Spirit of God.[2]

If we are consumed with the desire to accomplish 'the greater
works' promised by Jesus Christ, then no other alternative exists
but a return to the methods and means prescribed by God Himself. Repentance must be forthcoming for the neglect of the truth
and the power of the Spirit of God.

By way of personal reflection I must say that it has been painful
for me to acknowledge my woefully inadequate understanding of
the ministry of the Holy Spirit. To be brutally honest, over the
years my concern has been directed more toward avoiding
charismatic excesses than it has been toward rightfully
acknowledging the sovereign Spirit as He presents Himself on
the pages of His own scriptures. Consequently, the majority of
my efforts in pneumatology have been devoted to establishing

what the Spirit does not do, almost to the complete exclusion of establishing the magnificence of His person and the indispensability of His ministry in any positive way. Several years ago an old country preacher once described a group of Christians in a manner that would be appropriate to many of us today: 'They're as straight as a gun barrel ... but just as empty.' I am in no way promoting the idea that gospel preachers need to be any less straight. Do not misunderstand the emphasis. I am saying that it is essential for us to put a round in the chamber; in other words, that our ministries will never realize the fruitfulness we desire until our understanding of the Holy Spirit and His work transcends mere orthodox expressions of what He does not do.

The Spirit Of Truth

The scriptures define the Holy Spirit to be a person, a fact to which we will give some detailed consideration in a future chapter. Moreover, the scriptures clearly present the Holy Spirit as a divine person, possessing all the qualities of Godhood. At this juncture, however, it is a third and much overlooked truth concerning the Holy Spirit that needs to occupy our attention; namely, that the Holy Spirit is the communicator of divine truth. This fact can be easily established from many different perspectives, but the most obvious is to be found in the name that Jesus Christ assigns to Him: 'And I will ask the Father, and He will give you another Helper, that He may be with you forever; that is the *Spirit of truth* ...' (John 14:16-17), a name to which Jesus again refers on two subsequent occasions in this same discourse (15:26; 16:13).

Of all the revealed excellencies of God, that which theologians have referred to as God's 'veracity' has often proved to be a source of great comfort for His people. The God of the Bible is a God of integrity. He will not lie because He cannot lie. He is always consistent with Himself, and everything He says is absolutely true and unquestionable. Moreover, this veracity is a divine perfection of each member of the triune Godhead: Father,

Son, and Holy Spirit. The burden of Jesus at this point, however, is not so much to emphasize the *essential nature* of the Holy Spirit. Rather, it is to stress the *unique action* of the Holy Spirit. In other words, not only is the Holy Spirit 'truth' in the essence of His being; the emphasis here is upon the Holy Spirit as the *source* of truth, *the deliverer* of truth, the One who will *make known* the truth.[3] He is the sacred communicator.

Of course, the description of the Holy Spirit initially given by Jesus in this text is the term $\pi\alpha\rho\alpha\kappa\lambda\eta\tau\sigma\varsigma$. It is a generic word that means 'one who helps'.[4] In pre-Christian and extra-Christian literature it has been used to speak of an advocate[5] who would come alongside and support a defendant. It has been used to refer to a mediator.[6] Packer suggests it has no adequate English translation: '... it means by turns Comforter (in the sense of Strengthener), Counselor, Helper, Supporter, Adviser, Advocate, Ally, Senior Friend.'[7] But all of these varied usages beg an obvious question: how does one determine the meaning of this term in light of its evident elasticity? Clearly, the contexts in which this term is used press their own meaning into it. Such is the case in the present text. To be sure, the Holy Spirit helps the believer in many ways. But here it is something more particular that Jesus has in view. The help that the Holy Spirit is to bring to believers will come in the form of the communication of divine truth.

This communication occurs in two ways. First of all, the Spirit of God communicates His truth in an *objective and external* way; in a fashion that, properly considered, is non-experiential. Secondly, the Spirit of God communicates His truth to us in a *subjective and internal* way; in a fashion that is exceedingly experiential. It must be stressed that these are not two different bodies of truth, rather that our relationship to a single body of truth can be defined from two different perspectives. But it is necessary at this point to become more specific. How does the Holy Spirit communicate truth to us? *Objectively and externally, by the means of the inspiration of the Scripture.*

We believe the Bible to be the objective revelation of God.

We do not believe that the Bible merely contains thoughts about God. Nor do we affirm that God's true word is contained somewhere within the interior of the larger word. We believe that every page of scripture is a revelation of the mind of God, and that even the tenses of the verbs are an expression of His own breath. Moreover, our experience with or response to this objective revelation, whether positive or negative, has no bearing on its essential nature. William Still identifies the important distinction that exists between revelation and illumination:

> Revelation is what God has made known once and for all by the inspiration of his chosen writers; illumination is the work of the Spirit in bringing the truth of the 'closed book' to light. The art treasures of London's National Gallery remain intrinsically the same during the hours of darkness when they cannot be seen. We remain as essentially alive during the hours of unconsciousness in sleep as when we are awake. It is because we are alive that we can awake. It is surely a plain error of fact to say that the Bible 'becomes alive' in the divine-human encounter, when what we mean is that it awakes and shines forth its light and truth into the dark mind of man. The revelation of Christ in the Holy Scriptures is a work of God established long before we were born, and owes nothing to us, nor can it be subtracted from or added to by us. It is the 'word of the Lord which liveth and abideth for ever'.[8]

Who, then, was the agent of this divine communication? The Holy Spirit. It is the Apostle Paul who makes the well-known affirmation: 'All scripture is inspired by God ...' (2 Tim. 3:16). The Apostle Peter is even more definitive:

> But know this first of all, that no prophecy of scripture is a matter of one's own interpretation, for no prophecy was ever made by an act of human will, but men moved by the Holy Spirit spoke from God (2 Pet. 1:20-21).

The Holy Spirit was the divine communicator of the objective revelation we have come to regard as the sacred scriptures. In fact, it is the promise of divine inspiration, in seedling form, that

Jesus here gives to His disciples, a promise He develops more thoroughly in the following two chapters, as we will see. Suffice it to say that the Spirit of God, as the communicator of divine truth, would superintend fallible men to produce a written body of infallible communication.

The Holy Liaison

Unfortunately, it is at this very point that many evangelicals draw up short, believing that they have given full theological consideration to the Spirit's communicative ministry. They have failed to understand, however, that the vestiges of sin in a regenerated person still hamper one's ability to experience the benefits of the word of God. Thus, unless the Spirit of truth performs His immediate work of illumination in holy liaison with the scriptures, they will fail to produce supernatural effects. This is not to suggest that the words of the Bible cannot be defined and understood apart from this illuminating work.[9] It is to say that the power of the scriptures will fail to be experienced apart from this communicative ministry of the Spirit. Of course, this fact is built upon an essential presupposition; namely, that God has given His truth not merely to be amassed, but to be experienced. The word of God is not only a literary piece to be scrutinized, but a source of authority to which the human will is to yield assent. The old Puritan Matthew Henry captures this emphasis:

> To be led into a truth is more than barely to know it; it is to be intimately and experimentally acquainted with it; to be piously and strongly affected with it; not only to have the notion of it in our heads, but the relish and savour and power of it in our hearts.[10]

In this same vein Octavius Winslow writes:

> To believe that God's word is true, and on the strength of that belief to be willing to renounce all other dependence, and to rest simply and implicitly upon its revealed plan of salvation, is a blessed attainment – an attainment only to be realised by the power of the Holy Ghost; but to know it from a deep experience of its sanctifying

power, from the heartfelt preciousness and fulfilment of its promises, from its sustaining and soothing influence in sorrow, its all-
sufficient light in darkness and perplexity, to be brought to trust the
naked promise because God has spoken it, to believe, and to go
forward, because He has said it, is a still higher step in faith's lad-
der, and a more illustrious display of the grace and power of the
Spirit.[11]

At the outset of this chapter three contemporary methods of
ministry were cited as attempts at the work of God apart from
the truth and the power of the Spirit of God. It is at this point I
now suggest a fourth, in part, because of its obvious relationship
to the subject under consideration. It is a ministry methodology
to which those of us in Reformed traditions are particularly
susceptible; an approach to ministry that is solely directed to the
mind, defining spiritual success as the intellectual acquisition of
biblical and theological knowledge. 'Can he articulate the five
points of Calvinism?' 'Does he know the standard answers to
the difficult texts which appear to teach an unlimited atonement?'
'Is he committed to the regulative principle of worship?' One's
acumen in answering questions such as these can often become a
litmus test of spiritual growth. Let it be said that this is no attempt
at minimizing the importance of biblical and theological truth.
Spiritual maturity is not possible apart from such truth. But the
fact remains, it is possible for a Christian to possess a vast amount
of biblical and theological knowledge while at the same time
being altogether devoid of spiritual maturity.

Of course, this has immediate bearing on the preparation of
preachers and their sermons. Preachers ought never to approach
the scriptures with a mere token consideration that suggests, 'I've
got a sermon idea in my mind and a creative outline from which
to preach. All that remains to be found is a text to lend some
credibility to my ideas.' Instead, the burden of the preacher is to
experience the power of the scriptures in his own life before he
stands at the sacred desk. 'The Word must become flesh again;
the preacher must become the vehicle of the Holy Spirit, his
mind inspired and his heart inflamed by the truth he preaches.'[12]

It is this experience of truth that fires the motivation of the preacher. As he awakens on the Lord's Day it is this that leads him to conclude, 'This may be the most important message I have ever preached.'[13] John Owen exhorts:

> It is not to learn *the form of the doctrine of godliness,* but to get the *power* of it implanted in our souls. And this is an eminent means of our making a progress in the knowledge of the truth. To seek after mere *notions of truth,* without an endeavor after an *experience of its power* in our hearts, is not the way to increase our understanding in spiritual things. He alone is in a posture to learn from God who sincerely gives up his mind, conscience, and affections to the power and rule of what is revealed unto him. Men may have in their study of the scripture other ends also, as the profit and edification of others; *but if this conforming of their own souls unto the power of the word* be not fixed in the first place in their minds, they do not *strive lawfully nor will be crowned.*[14]

Stated simply, the Bible possesses its own resident life (cf. Heb. 4:12; 1 Pet. 1:23), but it does not always beget life. The Bible is not a magic book. It is efficacious only when it is accompanied by the operative power of the Holy Spirit. Herein, then, is the second way the Spirit of God communicates divine truth: *subjectively and internally, by directly applying the inspired scriptures to the human heart.*

> There is an especial work of the Spirit of God on the minds of men, communicating spiritual wisdom, light, and understanding unto them, necessary unto their discerning and apprehending aright the mind of God in his word, and the understanding of the mysteries of heavenly truth contained therein.[15]

Considered by many to be the premier theologian of the Holy Spirit, John Calvin has written, 'For as God alone is a fit witness of himself in his word, so also the word will not find acceptance in men's hearts before it is sealed by the inward testimony of the Spirit.'[16] John Owen refers to the Holy Spirit as the 'principle efficient cause'[17] of all spiritual understanding. The Puritan,

Richard Sibbes, addresses this same issue with helpful imagery:

> As the spirits in the arteries quicken the blood in the veins, so the
> Spirit of God goes along with the word, and makes it work .... The
> word is nothing without the Spirit; it is animated and quickened by
> the Spirit.[18]

At the risk of being misunderstood, it must be affirmed that the unaccompanied scriptures are not sufficient for life transformation. The word of God must be attended by the operative power of the Spirit of God if salvation and sanctification are to occur.

Devastating to the evangelical cause in the present day, however, is the tacit assumption that an exclusive choice needs to be made between the word and the Spirit. Quite evidently, some Christians have opted for the Spirit. Ecstatic experiences are then touted as the verification that they have received Him in fulness. Often accompanying this 'Holy Spirit emphasis' is a distaste for diligent Bible study. 'Exegesis is non-spiritual,' we are told. 'Doctrine is divisive.' 'Theology is irrelevant.'

In reaction, others of us have swung the pendulum hard in the opposite direction. 'All we need is the raw meat of the word,' our attitudes clearly imply. This often reveals itself in the manner in which seminaries train men for gospel ministry. Over a three year period an aspiring preacher is equipped to diagram Greek sentences, parse Hebrew verbs, and quote Calvin, Luther, and Hodge verbatim. What is disconcerting about this, (and this from a person committed to the development of all of these skills!), is that it is possible inadvertently to convey the impression that the key to understanding the mind of God is found in the acquisition of an arsenal of highly technical and scientific skills. Over time men may come to regard the scriptures the way a biology student regards his proverbial frog; as a thing to dissect, rather than a source from which to hear God's voice. Rarely are seminarians taught to pray and fast and weep for the subjective and internal illumination of the Holy Spirit in correspondence with their diligent efforts in the sacred text.

Several years ago, in defending the inspiration and inerrancy of the Bible, conservatives marshalled their arguments with great enthusiasm. Unfortunately, due to a lack of attention given to the internal testimony of the Spirit,[19] an evident imbalance[20] resulted along with with certain attendant consequences. To be sure, by most accounts the battle for biblical inerrancy was won. On the other hand, evangelicalism in its contemporary form would incline us to conclude that the battle for biblical sufficiency was lost.[21]

The disturbing disparity is apparent. Some of God's people have chosen the Spirit. Others have come down on the side of the scriptures. The problem, however, is that first choice is something akin to heat without light; the second choice more akin to light without heat. The point is this: we must stop putting asunder what God Himself has joined together. No choice of emphases are intended between Spirit and word. Christians must seek both in indivisible oneness. More particularly, we must look for the Spirit of the living God at work in, with, and through the written word of God.

Identifying The Deficiency

Why is this ministry of the Spirit necessary? Why is it that the objective and external revelation of God is insufficient to transform when unattended by the illuminating work of the Spirit of truth? Historically, the Roman Catholic Church has concluded that the problem of spiritual understanding lies in the nature of the scriptures themselves; namely, that they are obscure and fraught with perplexities. Hence, an ordinary man with a Bible in hand is sure to miscarry the truth. What, then, is the answer to his dilemma? An infallible interpreter, of course, the church itself.

The response of the Reformers and their followers was exceedingly clear: the problem in understanding the mind of God has nothing to do with the nature of the Bible. The communicator Himself is perfect and true. His communication in the scriptures was without flaw and is perspicuous. The problem in understanding the mind of God, therefore, has everything to do with humanity. The weak link in the communicative process is to be found in us. One need only give brief consideration to the scriptures in order to discover how definitively they speak concerning the capacities of fallen humanity:

the intent of man's heart is evil from his youth (Gen. 8:21).

the hearts of the sons of men are full of evil, and insanity is in their hearts throughout their lives (Ecc. 9:3).

the mind set on the flesh is hostile toward God; for it does not subject itself to the law of God, for it is not even able to do so (Rom. 8:7).

the Gentiles also walk, in the futility of their mind, being darkened in their understanding, excluded from the life of God, because of the ignorance that is in them, because of the hardness of their heart (Eph. 4:17-18).

to those who are defiled and unbelieving, nothing is pure, but both their mind and their conscience are defiled (Tit. 1:15).

In part, this is the very issue to which theologians refer when they speak of the doctrine of 'total depravity'. By this they do not mean to imply that any person is as wicked as he or she might be. Rather, they seek to make clear that sin has affected the totality of our humanness: heart, mind, will, conscience, affections, body. The Bible summarizes the condition of humankind in one pregnant phrase: 'And you were dead in your trespasses and sins' (Eph. 2:1).

Shortly after Lori and I were married we moved into a caretaker's apartment at a local mortuary where we lived for the next several months. Down the hall from our apartment was the embalming room where careful morticians prepared bodies for burial. Had I been so inclined, (hypothetically speaking!), to walk down the hall, enter that embalming room, and prick the big toe of one of those bodies with the sharp point of a safety pin, what kind of response could I have anticipated? No response at all, because the body possessed no capacity for responding to physical stimulation. In the same sense, a person spiritually dead possesses no capacity for responding to spiritual stimulation. Owen has stated it most graphically:

> ... the hearts of all men are fat, their ears heavy, and their eyes sealed, that they can neither hear, nor perceive, nor understand the mysteries of the kingdom of God. These things belong unto the work of the Holy Spirit upon our minds.[22]

To be sure, an unaided person can absorb the scriptures through his eyes and ears. On a purely intellectual level he may possess the mental faculties necessary to assimilate some of the concepts being communicated. He may even possess the skill to regurgitate it in some kind of responsive fashion. But to acknowledge that truth in his heart and conform to it in his will is altogether beyond his fallen capacities. He has been informed, but not illuminated. He has read words from a book called the Bible, but he has not heard the voice of God. This is the very point of the Apostle Paul: 'But a natural man does not accept the things of the Spirit of God; for they are foolishness to him, and he cannot understand them, because they are spiritually appraised' (1 Cor. 2:14). Hence, the indispensability of the Spirit's work becomes evident as man's depravity is properly understood. Pierre Marcel succinctly captures this concern:

> Scripture clearly teaches that there is an operation of the Spirit in the soul, an operation independent of the sanctifying influence of truth and necessary if that influence is to be effective .... He who is spiritually dead must be quickened by the almighty power of God before the things of the Spirit can have complete effect on him. He who is spiritually blind needs to have his sight restored before he can distinguish things which are revealed and offered by God. *Being independent of truth, this action cannot be imputed to the truth.* Hence, the innumerable prayers in scripture which refer to this specific work of the Spirit: prayer for God to change the hearts, open the eyes, unstop the ears of men; prayer that he will to give them ears to hear and eyes to see ... [23]

The deficiency in the process of spiritual understanding is not something inherent in the scriptures themselves, but endemic to the nature of fallen humanity. Consequently, immediate intervention of the Holy Spirit is essential if the power of truth is to be experienced.

A Striking Illustration

Consider the Jewish opponents of Jesus as they appear in the Gospels. Most certainly they were avid readers of the Old Testament scriptures. In all probability they possessed clear, working definitions of each Hebrew word. No doubt many, from firsthand experience, could rightly identify the various subtleties of semitic poetry. Yet, despite their skills, both native and acquired, they failed to understand the mind of God as revealed in their scriptures. 'How can you be so sure of this?' someone may ask. Even a cursory reading of the Gospels reveals the failure of the Jews to recognize the one Person to whom all of the Old Testament points. The indictment from the prologue of the fourth Gospel is indeed stunning: 'He came to His own, and those who were His own did not receive Him' (John 1:11). Sometime later Jesus provided an explanation for this rejection:

> 'No man can come to Me, unless the Father who sent Me draws him; and I will raise him up on the last day. It is written in the prophets, "And they shall all be taught of God" ' (John 6:44-45a).

But, it must be asked, who are these 'all' who are 'taught of God?' Jesus answers that question in the following line: 'Everyone who has heard and learned from the Father, comes to Me' (John 6:45). Those who are 'God-taught' readily embrace the revelation of God in His Son, Jesus Christ. It is essential, moreover, to notice two additional facts concerning this spiritual instruction: (1) it is sovereign in expression; and (2) it is divine in origin. These same two facts are made evident by Jesus elsewhere: '... no one knows the Son, except the Father; nor does anyone know the Father except the Son, and anyone to whom the Son wills to reveal Him' (Matt. 11:27).

This is how the gospel advances. This is God's method and means: truth and power. People are brought to faith in Jesus Christ not because a preacher happens to be exceptionally dynamic one Sunday morning, or because he finishes his sermon with a spellbinding story. Rather, in a mysterious work that is both sovereign in expression and divine in origin,[24] the power of God unites with the proclamation of the word of God and produces effects that are in keeping with the purposes of God. It is the effectual teaching ministry of the Spirit of truth, without which the Bible will never be anything more than a book in a drawer in a room at a hotel.

Of course, it must be acknowledged that what is essential in the experience of an unbeliever continues to be necessary in the life of the regenerate person. For the truth of God's word to be grasped, the Holy Spirit must continue to teach the child of God. Thus, Marcel rightly states:

> His action is not limited to the single act which produces the initial change of regeneration, after which the renewed soul would be abandoned to the pure and simple action of truth and of the commandments of God. The action of the Spirit is continual and cannot be compared with a uniformly acting force co-operating with truth. It is manifested more at one moment than at another, sometimes in one way, sometimes in another. The help and intervention of the Spirit may be invoked and implored; it is possible to grieve the Spirit and to resist him.[25]

It is for this very reason the Apostle Paul prays for believers:[26]

> I ... do not cease giving thanks for you, while making mention of you in my prayers; that the God of our Lord Jesus Christ, the Father of glory, may give to you a spirit of wisdom and of revelation in the knowledge of Him. I pray that the eyes of your heart may be enlightened, so that you may know what is the hope of His calling, what are the riches of the glory of His inheritance in the saints, and what is the surpassing greatness of His power toward us who believe (Eph. 1:15-19).

Be it evangelistic or edificational, the context makes no difference. For the truth to be known, the Spirit of God must draw His sword.

Notes

1. For excerpts of this address see Iain H. Murray, *D. Martyn Lloyd-Jones* (Carlisle: The Banner of Truth Trust, 1990), vol. II, pp. 300-301.

2. *Ibid.*, p. 292.

3. The construction of πνεῦμα τῆς ἀληθείας (the Spirit of truth) is an objective genitive, *i.e.* the noun in the genitive (ἀληθείας) acts as the object or receives the action implied in the noun on which it depends (πνεῦμα). Certainly this can be implied from the other Paraclete passages (14:26; 15:26; 16:12-15). 'In other words, the Spirit of truth is the Spirit who communicates truth.' D. A. Carson, *The Farewell Discourse and Final Prayer of Jesus* (Grand Rapids: Baker Book House, 1980), p. 52.

4. Johannes P. Louw and Eugene A. Nida, *Greek-English Lexicon of the New Testament Based on Semantic Domains* (New York: United Bible Societies, 1989), vol. I, p. 142.

5. G. Abbott Smith, *A Manual Greek Lexicon of the New Testament* (Edinburgh: T & T Clark, 1981), p. 340.

6. William F. Arndt and F. Wilbur Gingrich, *A Greek-English Lexicon of the New Testament and Other Early Christian Literature* (Chicago: The University of Chicago Press, 1979), p. 618.

7. J. I. Packer, *Keep in Step with the Spirit* (Old Tappan: Fleming H. Revell Company, 1984), p. 61.

8. William Still, 'The Holy Spirit in Preaching', *Christianity Today* (Sept. 2, 1957), pp. 8-9.

9. '... the word of God is spiritual, which means that it is appropriated by spiritual means. It is a rational word, which means that the human reason is involved in its appropriation. But as a spiritual word something more is required, such as faith, meditation, prayer, and obedience. On the divine side, the word is assisted by the Holy Spirit ... people who are not Christians may read and understand Holy Scripture and books of Christian theology at the level of rational communication. Christian revelation is not in an odd language or composed of hidden or esoteric symbols. But the perception of the text of scripture as the word of God can be had only when, in addition to the rational criterion, spiritual criteria are used.' Bernard Ramm, *After Fundamentalism* (San Francisco: Harper & Row Publishers, 1983), p. 96.

10. Matthew Henry, *Matthew Henry's Commentary On The Whole Bible* (repr. ed., Peabody: Hendrickson Publishers, 1994), vol. 5, p. 919.

11. Octavius Winslow, *The Work of the Holy Spirit* (repr. ed., Carlisle:

The Banner of Truth Trust, 1991), pp. 155-156.

12. Still, 'The Holy Spirit', p. 9.

13. 'The Princeton leaders had consciously faced the key question: What was it that gave life to plain, scriptural preaching? And their united answer was, it was preachers knowing and feeling in their own experience the realities of which they spoke.' Iain Murray, *Revival and Revivalism* (Carlisle: The Banner of Truth Trust, 1994), p. 45.

14. John Owen, *The Works of John Owen* (repr. ed., Carlisle: The Banner of Truth Trust), vol. 4, pp. 205-206.

15. *Ibid.*, p. 124.

16. John Calvin, *Institutes of the Christian Religion* (repr. ed., Philadelphia: The Westminster Press, 1960), vol. 1, p. 79.

17. Owen, *Works,* vol. 4, p. 124.

18. Richard Sibbes, *Works of Richard Sibbes* (repr. ed., Carlisle: The Banner of Truth Trust, 1978), vol. 7, p. 199.

19. Admittedly, all mention of the internal testimony of the Spirit was not ignored. As stated by the International Council on Biblical Inerrancy, 'The Holy Spirit, Scripture's divine author, both authenticates it to us by His inward witness and opens our minds to understand its meaning.' *Chicago Statement on Biblical Inerrancy* (Oakland: International Council on Biblical Inerrancy, 1978), par. 3. Nevertheless, since the time of the Fundamentalist-Liberal controversy in the 1920s, the vast majority of literature written to defend the integrity of the scriptures has given only token consideration to this ministry of the Spirit.

20. Related to this issue are the words of Martyn Lloyd-Jones as he addressed the imbalance of intellectualism in Reformed preaching: 'I want to say a word in defence of the Orthodox Presbyterian Church and Westminster Seminary. In the 1920s the liberal movement possessed great power and made inroads everywhere in the Presbyterian Church. These conservative men were driven into a defensive position, so when they came to form a seminary the uppermost idea was the defence of the Faith, to establish a bulwark of orthodoxy. The fundamentalist was also defending the faith, but in an unintelligent way. It had to be done in an intelligent manner, with more scholarship and more learning ... it was almost inevitable that a lack of balance should occur, and a lack of vitality and power in the propagation of the gospel. We must not allow the situation we are in to determine what we are and become. We should be masters of the situation, not victims of it. We can all easily be jockeyed into a false position by circumstances and by other people. We must be firmly in control, with our position controlled by the New Testament. This was the great lesson I learned in five months in America.' Murray, *D. Martyn Lloyd-Jones,* vol. 2, p. 620.

21. Most evangelical denominations and churches readily affirm their

commitment to the doctrine of biblical inspiration, and even biblical inerrancy. Ironically, however, many of these same denominations and churches stake their advancement upon humanly-devised methodologies to accomplish the work of God in the world.

22. Owen, *Works,* vol. 4, p. 124.

23. Pierre Ch. Marcel, *The Relevance of Preaching* (Grand Rapids: Baker Book House, 1963), p. 28.

24. Charles Bridges refers to this as 'the sovereign dispensation of divine influence'. Charles Bridges, *The Christian Ministry* (repr. ed., Carlisle: The Banner of Truth Trust, 1991), p. 80.

25. Marcel, *Relevance,* p. 28.

26. It is also helpful to take notice of the diverse and repeated petitions for spiritual understanding on the part of David in Psalm 119, a man in whom the Spirit clearly dwelt; *e.g.* 'Open my eyes, that I may behold wonderful things from Thy law' (Ps. 119:18). The same can be implied from the high-priestly prayer of Jesus as He petitions His Father for the work of sanctifying believers through the instrumentality of the word: 'Sanctify them in the truth; Thy word is truth' (John 17:17). See Arturo G. Azurdia III, *The Sanctifying Word* (Pleasant Hill: GSTM Publications, 1997), pp. 11-12.

3

THE CHRISTOCENTRIC SPIRIT

The scriptures should be read with the aim of finding Christ in them.
JOHN CALVIN

The Holy Spirit is ardent to reveal the Christ.
PIERRE MARCEL

The highest point of revelation should be the perspective from which
all revelation before and after that event should be seen.
BERNARD RAMM

To Reveal And Glorify Jesus Christ

How should clear-headed Christians regard the many and diverse
activities that are presently being claimed in the name of the
Holy Spirit? Of course, some would suggest that to even pose
such a question is irreverent at best, blasphemous at worst. To
the contrary, truth invites scrutiny. Only error fears close
examination. So, again I ask, what are we to think about the current
claims of phenomenal experiences that are being ascribed to the
Spirit of God? For example, some believers apparently speak in
ecstatic languages as a consequence of the Spirit's ministry. Others
claim to hear the audible voice of the Holy Spirit. Certain
Christians affirm multiple encounters of His baptizing work. Still
others stake their ministries on 'Spirit-given' prophecies
regarding the future. On occasion I have observed a well-known
'faith-healer' remove his suit coat and wave it across the front
of an audience. As a result, hundreds of people fall to the ground;
all, we are assured, as an affirmation of the Spirit's presence
and power. In fact, it is not uncommon for this same man to turn

his attention toward a pre-selected individual and shout 'Boo!', thus knocking him backwards into the arms of waiting, well-placed men. Displays such as these are described as definitive verifications of the Spirit's 'anointing' on the healer himself. Though amazing to some, these are not unusual phenomena. They can be observed daily and nightly on Christian television in America. Moreover, it appears that an evolution in the intensity of these phenomena is taking place; an evolution toward greater excessiveness. We now hear of Christians 'barking' in the Spirit, 'laughing' in the Spirit, and even 'vomiting' in the Spirit.

Two serious concerns should be aroused within us related to these 'Holy Spirit experiences'. Firstly, from a *pastoral* perspective, we need to be concerned that the spiritual development of well-meaning Christians can become vulnerable to the law of diminishing returns. That is to say, the maturing of a Christian will be consistently impaired if devotion to Jesus Christ is determined by fresh experiences of spiritual ecstasy. Why is this the case? Because one's sensation of being overpowered by God will need to steadily intensify. The ordinary will give way to the unusual. The unusual will surrender to the extreme. The extreme will topple to the ridiculous. Often, the inevitable consequence is spiritual emptiness.

So the seeker for experience goes back through the ritual again and again, but begins to discover something; ecstatic experience, like drug-addiction, requires larger and larger doses to satisfy. Sometimes the bizarre is introduced. I have seen people run around a room until they were exhausted, climb tent poles, laugh hysterically, go into trances for days and do other weird things as the 'high' sought became more elusive. Eventually there is a crisis and a decision is made; he will sit on the back seats and be a spectator, 'fake it', or go on in the hope that everything will eventually be as it was. The most tragic decision is to quit and in the quitting abandon all things spiritual as fraudulent. The spectators are frustrated, the fakers suffer guilt, the hoping are pitiable and the quitters are a tragedy.[1]

Secondly, there is a *doctrinal/theological* concern that ought to unsettle us regarding these much sought-after enthusiasms; namely, that the ministry of the Holy Spirit has become Christian-centered rather than Christ-centered.[2] At this very point a great deal of contemporary evangelicalism steadily reveals its failure to recognize the predominant ministry of the Holy Spirit. To be sure, many seriously-minded Christians are deeply confused regarding the Spirit's ministry. The aforementioned excesses have aroused puzzlement. Some have given up all attempts at any discriminating thinking. While it is true that many may never become thorough-going experts in the field of pneumatology, there is an interpretive question to which every Christian can ask of any ministry purporting to be a work of the Holy Spirit: *Does this ministry reveal and glorify Jesus Christ?* This is the holy ambition of the Spirit of God. Concerning the purpose of the Spirit's imminent advent Jesus said: 'He shall glorify Me ...' (John 16:14a). J. I. Packer illustrates the relationship between the Son and the Spirit as follows:

I remember walking to a church one winter evening to preach on the words 'He shall glorify Me,' seeing the building floodlit as I turned a corner, and realizing that this was exactly the illustration my message needed. When floodlighting is well done, the floodlights are so placed that you do not see them; you are not in fact supposed to see where the light is coming from; what you are meant to see is just the building on which the floodlights are trained. The intended effect is to make it visible when otherwise it would not be seen for the darkness, and to maximize its dignity by throwing all its details into relief so that you see it properly. This perfectly illustrates the Spirit's new covenant role. He is, so to speak, the hidden floodlight shining on the Savior. Or think of it this way. It is as if the Spirit stands behind us, throwing light over our shoulder, onto Jesus, who stands facing us. The Spirit's message to us is never, 'Look at Me; listen to Me; come to Me; get to know Me,' but always, 'Look at *Him*, and see His glory; listen to *Him*, and hear His word; go to *Him*, and have His life; get to know *Him*, and taste His gift of joy and peace.' The Spirit, we might say, is the matchmaker, the celestial marriage broker, whose role it is to bring us and Christ together and ensure that we stay together. As the second Paraclete, the Spirit leads us constantly to the original Paraclete, Jesus, who Himself draws near through the second Paraclete's coming to us. Thus, by enabling us to discern the first Paraclete, and by moving us to stretch out our hands to Him as He comes from His throne to meet us, the Holy Spirit glorifies Christ, according to Christ's own word.[3]

Jesus has already referred to the Holy Spirit as 'the Spirit of truth' (John 14:17). As we have seen, this has reference to the Spirit's communicative ministry. It should be noted, moreover, that coming so soon after the claim of Jesus to be 'the truth' (John 14:6), this may more particularly define the indwelling Spirit as the One who communicates the truth *concerning Jesus*. This is stated more emphatically by Jesus Himself as His discourse continues:

> But the Helper, the Holy Spirit, whom the Father will send in My name, He will teach you all things, and bring to your remembrance *all that I said to you* (John 14:26).

> When the Helper comes, whom I will send to you from the Father, that is the Spirit of truth, who proceeds from the Father, *He will bear witness of Me* (John 15:26).[4]

> But when He, the Spirit of truth, comes, He will guide you into all the truth; for He will not speak on His own initiative, but whatever He hears, He will speak; and He will disclose to you what is to come. *He shall glorify Me*; for He shall take of Mine, and shall disclose it to you. All things that the Father has are Mine; therefore I said, that He takes of Mine, and will disclose it to you (John 16:13-15).

There can be no confusion regarding these words. Jesus will be the sum and substance of the Spirit's revelatory ministry. The predominant work of the Holy Spirit is to reveal and glorify Jesus Christ, a fact of which we must never lose sight if we are ever to anticipate the Holy Spirit's power.

The Christ-Centered Scriptures

How does the Holy Spirit reveal and glorify Jesus Christ? He does so in a multiplicity of ways. For example, the Holy Spirit glorifies Jesus Christ by making people aware of their need for a Savior. No person rightly regards the Son of God until he is brought to a recognition of his sinful condition. In addition, the Holy Spirit glorifies Jesus Christ by revealing the saving sufficiency of His redemptive work. To be sure, many who are not Christians can rightly articulate the basis for the Christian faith: the crucifixion and resurrection of Jesus Christ. However, when the Spirit of God supernaturally opens the eyes of those previously blind, the historical events of redemption are infused with personal meaning and value. Consequently, they draw out an eager response of repentance and faith. Moreover, the Holy Spirit glorifies Jesus Christ in the life of a believer by progressively revealing the beauty and excellencies of His person and work. Of course, with little effort we could add to this list. What is important, however, is the realization that the many and varied ways by which the Spirit glorifies Jesus Christ come to us through the means of one particular channel: the written word of God which, from cover to cover, sets forth one great and glorious person, Jesus Christ.[5]

Evangelicals must cease to think of the Bible as an inspired book of virtues. It is not primarily a God-breathed manual for piloting our way through life successfully. Rather, it is a book that is concerned to make known the plight of humanity and the purpose of God to save humanity through His Son. Jesus Christ is promised within the earliest pages of the Bible. The middle of the Bible provides a historical account of His coming and accomplishments. At the end of the Bible Jesus Christ is set forth as the glorious object of worship for all the created order throughout eternity. To be sure, these are the great and mighty pillars upon which the whole of biblical revelation rests. It must be recognized with equal verve, however, that every other portion of sacred scripture reinforces this redemptive superstructure.[6] The Bible is a record of the redemption of the people of God by His Son, Jesus Christ. Hence:

If one is looking primarily for a book of stories designed to teach a moral lesson, the Bible may not be as good as Aesops' fables. All of the biblical heroes represent sinfulness, disobedience, half-heartedness and pride as well as faith and obedience. The real hero is God, who remains faithful to His promise in spite of human sin. No, moral instruction comes easily to us, but the gospel is not in us by nature; it must be revealed from heaven. This is chiefly why we have the word of God. To preach the Bible as 'the handbook for life,' or as the answer to every question, rather than as a revelation of Christ, is to turn the Bible into an entirely different book. This is how the Pharisees approached scripture; however, as we can see clearly from the questions they asked Jesus, all of them amounting to something akin to *Trivial Pursuits*: 'What happens if a person divorces and remarries?' 'Why do your disciples pick grain on the Sabbath?' 'Who sinned – this man or his parents – that he was born blind?' For the Pharisees, the scriptures were a source of trivia for life's dilemmas. To be sure, scripture provides God-centered and divinely-revealed wisdom for life, but if this were its primary objective, Christianity would be a religion of self-improvement by following examples and exhortations, not a religion of the Cross.[7]

John Calvin concluded:

The scriptures should be read with the aim of finding Christ in them. Whoever turns aside from this object, even though he wears himself out all of his life in learning, he will never reach the knowledge of the truth.[8]

Consider Spurgeon's well-known exhortation to an aspiring preacher:

Don't you know, young man, that from every town and every village and every hamlet in England, wherever it may be, there is a road that leads to London? ... So from every text in scripture there is a road towards the great metropolis, Christ. And my dear brother, your business is, when you get to a text, to say, now what is the road that leads to Christ? ... the sermon cannot do any good unless there is a savour of Christ in it.[9]

To reveal and glorify Jesus Christ is the predominant ministry of the Holy Spirit. How does He accomplish this aim? Through the means of the inscripturated word which centers its focus on Jesus Christ. Closer scrutiny of the statements of Jesus reveals something of their comprehensiveness concerning this Christocentric emphasis. For example, Jesus says of the Spirit: 'He will ... bring to your remembrance all that I said to you' (John 14:26). This 'word of remembrance' is inscripturated in the narrative portions of the New Testament; those portions which record the words and works of Jesus Christ (Matthew–Acts). But the New Testament also sets forth the theologizing of the truth of Jesus in both its doctrinal and ethical outworking; revelation embodied in the epistolary literature of the New Testament (Romans–Jude). The promise of the Spirit will include this work of inspiration as well: '... when He, the Spirit of truth, comes, He will guide you into all the truth' (John 16:13). The definite article ('all the truth') suggests, not that the Spirit will guide the apostles into the truth regarding all subjects; rather that He will guide them into the specific truth about the person of Jesus and the significance of His work.[10] Finally, the New Testament is inclusive of truth concerning Jesus that is prophetic (*e.g.* the book of Revelation). The Spirit, promises Jesus, will speak concerning the future: 'He will disclose to you what is to come' (John 16:13).[11] This, then, is Christ's pre-authentication of the New Testament scriptures. The promised Holy Spirit will glorify Jesus Christ by guiding the apostles into all truth concerning Jesus Christ.

> This means that the Holy Spirit does not testify by the written word anything against Christ, the incarnate Word. The two are never in opposition to each other, but always bear witness to each other. The written word is the divinely inspired revelation concerning the incarnate Word, the Saviour of sinners, by which the Holy Spirit is operative toward their salvation.[12]

Of course, at this point most Christians would be in agreement: the principle subject of the New Testament scriptures is Jesus Christ. But how are Christians to regard the Old Testament scriptures? 'Certainly,' some would suggest, 'there are a few texts in the Old Testament that make allusion to Jesus Christ. But, the fact is, the majority of these scriptures say nothing of him.' Does this commonly held perspective stand the scrutiny of New Testament revelation? Perhaps fresh consideration needs to be given to the inspired perspective of the apostolic authors. Consider Paul:

> You, however, continue in the things you have learned and become convinced of, knowing from whom you have learned them; and that from childhood you have known the sacred writings which are able to give you the wisdom that leads to salvation through faith which is in Christ Jesus (2 Tim. 3:14-15).

The 'sacred writings' were what we have now come to possess as the Old Testament scriptures. These are at the heart of Paul's affirmation in the following verse: 'All scripture is inspired by God ...' (2 Tim. 3:16). But what purpose do these scriptures serve for people living in the epoch of New Testament? Paul is exceedingly clear: 'which are able to give you the wisdom that leads to salvation through faith which is in Christ Jesus.' This fact would prove stunning to many contemporary evangelicals. 'The *Old Testament* can lead a person to faith in Jesus Christ?' They most certainly can, when we interpret them as they were intended to be interpreted; that is, not merely as texts in isolation from the rest of the Bible, but as signposts in anticipation of the redemption that was to be accomplished by the Son of God. The Apostle Peter writes:

> As to this salvation, the prophets who prophesied of the grace that would come to you made careful search and inquiry, seeking to know what person or time the Spirit of Christ within them was indicating as he predicted the sufferings of Christ and the glories to follow. It was revealed to them that they were not serving them-selves, but you, in these things which now have been announced to you through those who preached the gospel to you by the Holy Spirit sent from heaven – things into which angels long to look (1 Pet. 1:10-12).

Two questions should be asked at this point. Firstly, who was the source of this revelation, giving to these prophets what has come to comprise the Old Testament scriptures? The 'Spirit of Christ within them.' Secondly, to what and to whom was the Spirit of Christ pointing through these prophets? Initially, Peter speaks of 'this salvation'. He then refers to 'the grace that would come to you'. More definitively Peter says of the prophetic Spirit, 'He predicted the sufferings of Christ and the glories to follow.' In other words, the Spirit who inspired the writings of the New Testament, which *reflectively* center upon the person and work of Jesus Christ, is the same Spirit who inspired the writings of the Old Testament, also focused upon Christ, but in an *anticipatory* fashion.

If Christians are to read the Bible rightly they must understand that the scriptures of the Old Testament are not a self-contained revelation. This is certainly Paul's clear implication in the introduction and benediction from his epistle to the Romans:

> Paul, a bond-servant of Christ Jesus, called as an apostle, set apart for the gospel of God, which he promised beforehand *through his prophets in the holy scriptures, concerning his Son,* who was born of a descendant of David according to the flesh .... Now to him who is able to establish you according to my gospel and the preaching of Jesus Christ, according to the revelation of the mystery which has been kept secret for long ages past, but now is manifested, and *by the scriptures of the prophets,* according to the commandment of the eternal God, has been made known to all the nations, leading to obedience of faith; to the only wise God, through Jesus Christ, be the glory forever. Amen (Rom. 1:1-3; 16:25-27).

Thus, Ramm contends for the following:

> ... the highest point of revelation (for Ramm this is the incarnation of God in Jesus Christ, John 1:14) should be the perspective from which all revelation before and after that event should be seen. By analogy, a sailboat is built up board by board. But the design was not made up as the boards were set in place. The complete drafted plans were in hand before one board was laid hold of. Hence the

finished draft of the ship guides the placement of every board. The incarnation of God in Christ is like the finished draft of the ship. The Old Testament in anticipation of the incarnation was so written as to prepare the way for the incarnation. Hence it is not wrong to bring Christ into the Old Testament, because ... the Old Testament was written Christologically .... If the Old Testament is not a Christian book, then it is a very odd book. It has many eschatological dimensions that anticipate some great action of God in the future – a kingdom of God, a new covenant, a Messiah, a resurrection from the dead. If the Old Testament is understood only as a body of ethical, national, and cultic teachings, then these eschatological promises stick up like so many unfinished stumps asking for completion but being denied.[13]

It was for this reason the Old Testament became the Bible for the early Christians; not because they assumed it could serve to supply some moral guidelines until the New Testament could be written. Rather, they were persuaded that the Old Testament scriptures pointed them to Jesus Christ, to the days of fulfillment when all the pictures, shadows, types, and promises of redemption would be accomplished in Him. Consider the testimony of Philip, proclaimed during the earliest days of Jesus' public ministry:

The next day he purposed to go forth into Galilee, and he found Philip. And Jesus said to him, 'Follow Me.' Now Philip was from Bethsaida, of the city of Andrew and Peter. Philip found Nathanael and said to him, *'We have found Him of whom Moses in the Law and also the Prophets wrote, Jesus of Nazareth,* the son of Joseph' (John 1:43-45).

Philip embraces the comprehensiveness of Old Testament revelation when he refers to 'the Law and also the Prophets' as writing of Jesus. Jesus Himself said to the Pharisees:

'You search the scriptures, because you think that in them you have eternal life; and it is these that bear witness of Me.... Do not think that I will accuse you before the Father; the one who accuses you is Moses, in whom you have set your hope. For if you believed Moses, you would believe Me; for he wrote of Me' (John 5:39, 45-46).

In his sermon on the Day of Pentecost Peter quotes from 2 Samuel 7, Psalms 16 and 110, and Joel 2. In Acts 3, when Peter preaches the gospel in the temple, he explains: 'But the things which God announced beforehand by the mouth of all the prophets, that His Christ should suffer, He has thus fulfilled' (Acts 3:18). As his sermon unfolds he quotes Genesis 22 and Deuteronomy 18. Preaching before the Sanhedrin in Acts 4 Peter quotes Psalm 118. In Acts 8 Philip preaches Christ to an Ethiopian eunuch from the text of Isaiah 53. When Peter meets the God-fearer, Cornelius, he cites the Old Testament as his authority: 'Of Him all the prophets bear witness that through His name everyone who believes in Him receives forgiveness of sins' (Acts 10:43). Clearly, it was the apostolic pattern to preach Jesus Christ from the Old Testament. Not surprisingly, this proved to be the approach of Paul as well. After arriving in Thessalonica Luke records:

> ... he went to them, and for three Sabbaths reasoned with them from the scriptures, explaining and giving evidence that the Christ had to suffer and rise again from the dead, and saying, 'This Jesus whom I am proclaiming to you is the Christ' (Acts 17:2-3).

Later, in his defence before King Agrippa, Paul says:

> 'And so, having obtained help from God, I stand to this day testifying both to small and great, stating nothing but what the Prophets and Moses said was going to take place, that the Christ was to suffer, and that by reason of His resurrection from the dead He should be the first to proclaim light both to the Jewish people and to the Gentiles' (Acts 26:22-23).

Finally, as the book of Acts draws to a close, Paul is under house arrest in a Roman prison. Luke indicates that a large number of people came to see him. His approach is expectedly consistent:

> 'and he was explaining to them by solemnly testifying about the kingdom of God, and trying to persuade them concerning Jesus, from both the Law of Moses and from the Prophets, from morning until evening' (Acts 28:23).

Throughout the book of Acts the apostolic exposition of the Old Testament steadily points to Jesus Christ. These men were convinced that this was the Spirit-intended purpose of the Old Testament scriptures. Of course, this should not be surprising to us. The ministry of Jesus began with much the same emphasis. In the synagogue at Nazareth He stands, having taken the scroll of Isaiah in His hands, and He reads from the 61st chapter of that prophecy. As He finishes, He closes up the scroll, hands it back to the attendant, and sits down. And then, with every eye riveted upon Him, He says: 'Today this scripture has been fulfilled in your hearing' (Luke 4:21). In other words, 'Isaiah wrote of Me.'

We, too, must affirm that all of the scriptures are Christian. Until we read them in a Christic way, the purpose of the Spirit in giving them will elude us.[14]

A Personal Awakening

When I scan my Christian pilgrimage, I can quickly identify the three most significant high points. The first is my conversion. God saved me when I was twenty years old. The second is the evening God's Spirit opened my eyes to see the implications of the doctrines of grace. It felt as though I had been saved a second time. The third occurred a few years ago when I enrolled in a class at Westminster Seminary taught by Dr. Edmund Clowney. It was entitled, 'Preaching Christ from the Old Testament.'

Admittedly, I began the class with my resistance level turned up to full capacity. 'Never preach Christ if He is not specifically mentioned in the text from which you are preaching,' I had always heard. And yet for three hours each day Dr. Clowney showed us, from both exegetical and theological perspectives, how the Old Testament ruthlessly points to Jesus Christ. Each day I left class saying to my roommate, 'I love Jesus more today than I have ever before loved Him.' Without sounding hopelessly sentimental, it was something akin to an Emmaus road experience. Each day my heart would burn.

Equally unexpected, however, was the deep humility that accompanied this fresh experience of joy. After the second or third day into the class a painful realization broke open in my consciousness: *though I had been preaching the Bible expositionally for eleven years, I had altogether missed the Spirit-intended purpose of the first two-thirds of it!* Even more to the point was the lingering memory of a recently concluded twelve-part series on the book of Nehemiah. As diligently as I tried I failed to recollect one occasion of speaking about Jesus Christ during those twelve weeks of preaching, save for the mention of His name in my closing prayer at the conclusion of the sermon. And the haunting question which forcibly impressed itself upon my mind was this: *how can I ask for the Holy Spirit's power in preaching when I am completely out of step with the Holy Spirit's purpose in His word?* I was soon to discover that this question had been addressed by many to whom I needed to listen.

> This is the design that He (the Holy Spirit) is sent upon, this is the work that he comes to do; even as it was the design and work of Jesus Christ to glorify the Father, by whom He was sent. And this are they always to bear in mind who stand in need of or pray for his assistance in their work or office in the church of God: He is given unto them, that through him they may give and bring glory to Jesus Christ.[15] (parenthesis mine)

> And now, brethren, let me lay before you some reasons and motives, to back this friendly admonition concerning preaching Christ .... It is the only way to have our labours accepted of Christ, and to have communion with him in our work .... Even Paul cries out, 'Who is sufficient for these things?' With how much more reason may we do so? Does not our cheerful progress in our work depend on a divine *afflatus*, and the spirit dispensed by Christ? But if we take little notice of him in our preaching, and do not distinguish ourselves from the moral philosophers of the Gentiles, how can we expect any more of this enlivening and encouraging presence of Christ than they had? Nay, we have less ground to expect it, if we slight wilfully so noble a revelation, with which they were never favoured.[16]

It is often lamented that the Holy Spirit is the least understood Person of the Trinity, but surely we see why this is so; for the Holy Spirit comes not to speak of himself, but to glorify Christ. Where preachers are intent on glorifying Christ (and only crucified men can do so!), the Spirit is there with all his aid. All true showing forth of Christ is by the Holy Spirit.[17]

I have become convinced that preachers can rightly anticipate the Holy Spirit's power only when they are resolutely wedded to the Holy Spirit's purpose. What is His purpose? To glorify Jesus Christ through the instrumentality of the Old and the New Testament scriptures, both of which point to Him.

A Final Consideration

Of the many interpretive signals which lead to a Christological understanding of the Old Testament, one stands out as the most beneficial. It appears in the final chapter of the Gospel of Luke. There the resurrected Savior rebukes two discouraged disciples. The basis for His reproach? Their failure to understand the Old Testament scriptures:

'O foolish men and slow of heart to believe in all that the prophets have spoken! Was it not necessary for the Christ to suffer these things and to enter into His glory?' And beginning with Moses and with all the prophets, He explained to them the things concerning Himself in all the scriptures (Luke 24:25-27).

Their hearts burn as a consequence of seeing Christ in all of the scriptures. Sometime later that day Jesus appears to the larger group of disciples. After displaying the true humanity of His resurrected body, He continues with the same kind of instruction begun earlier on the Emmaus road:

'These are My words which I spoke to you while I was still with you, that all things which are written about Me in the Law of Moses and the Prophets and the Psalms must be fulfilled.' Then He opened their minds to understand the scriptures, and He said to them, 'Thus it is written, that the Christ should suffer and rise again from the dead the third day ...' (Luke 24:44-46).

Here Jesus draws upon the totality of Old Testament revelation, the three major divisions of the Hebrew scriptures: the Law, the Prophets, and the Psalms. Clowney states:

> The phrase 'beginning at Moses and all the prophets' and the use of the verb *diermeneuo* indicate reasoned interpretation. Jesus did not present a course in 'eisegesis'. He interpreted what the scriptures *do* say and opened His disciples' minds to understand it .... Although Jesus was their teacher, He did not assume that only He could so interpret scripture. Rather, He blamed them as fools and slow of heart because they had not perceived the plain meaning of the Old Testament. Indeed, so clear is the message of the scriptures that their misunderstanding must be accounted for by a mental block of some kind, a blindness to the truth expressed.[18]

The inscripturated word centers its attention on Jesus Christ. He is the seed of the woman who will crush the serpent's head. He is the ark to rescue the people of God. He is the holy Angel of Yahweh. He is the seed of Abraham in whom all the families of the earth will be blessed. He is the passover lamb. He is the prophet greater than Moses. He is the pillar of fire in the wilderness. He is the rock struck by Moses. He is the heir to the Davidic throne. He is the thrice holy Lord of Isaiah 6. He is the greater shepherd of Ezekiel 34. He is Mary's baby, Herod's enemy, and Simeon's joy. He is the twelve-year-old boy in the temple and the beloved Son to be baptized. He is the healer of the blind, the provider for the hungry, and the friend of the outcast. He is the new temple, the source of living water, the manna that gives life, the light of the world, the resurrection and the life, and the Father's true vine. He is the spotless lamb of God who takes away the sin of the world and the resurrected lion from the tribe of Judah. He is the ascended Lord, the ruler of the Church, and the returning Judge of all men. The sacred scriptures are the instrument by which the Spirit of the living God glorifies Jesus Christ.

But all of this raises one final question: how does the Spirit intend for this inscripturated word of Christ to be made known?

Answer: through preachers who, with the message of Christ on their lips, will be given divine power by this same Holy Spirit.

> 'Thus it is written, that the Christ should suffer and rise again from the dead the third day; and that repentance for forgiveness of sins should be proclaimed in His name to all the nations, beginning from Jerusalem. You are witnesses of these things. *And behold, I am sending forth the promise of My Father upon you; but you are to stay in the city until you are clothed with power from on high'* (Luke 24:46-49).

At this vital point, three essential principles of apostolic ministry converge: the message, method, and means for ministry ordained by Jesus Christ. *The divine message?* Jesus Christ. *The divine method?* Authoritative proclamation. *The divine means?* The power of the Spirit of God. This, then, summarizes that to which I am referring as 'the vitality of the Spirit'. In a single statement, *the vitality of the Spirit is His effectual work of glorifying Jesus Christ through fallible men who faithfully proclaim the Christocentric scriptures.* This is ministry distinctive to the new covenant people of God: Christ is our message, preaching Christ from all of the scriptures is our method, and the attending power of the purchased Spirit of God is our means. A deeper look into the New Testament will reveal that the practice of apostolic ministry was thoroughly consistent with this instruction of Jesus.

If ever we are to expect the Spirit's enablement, we must be resolutely wedded to His purpose; to glorify Jesus Christ through the instrumentality of the scriptures. When this message is our message we can look for His vitality. God's purposes will advance. Hearts will burn. Minds will be opened. People will come to know and love Jesus Christ.

> The Holy Ghost never sets His signature to a blank check ... the Holy Ghost will only bless in conformity with His own set purpose. Our Lord explains what that purpose is: 'He shall glorify Me.' He has come forth for this grand end, and He will not put up with anything short of it. If, then, we do not preach Christ, what is the Holy Ghost to do with

our preaching? If we do not make the Lord Jesus glorious; if we do not lift Him high in the esteem of men, if we do not labour to make Him King of kings, and Lord of lords; we shall not have the Holy Spirit with us. Vain will be rhetoric, music, architecture, energy, and social status: if our own design be not to magnify the Lord Jesus, we shall work alone and work in vain.[19]

Notes

1. George Gardiner, *The Corinthian Catastrophe* (Grand Rapids: Kregel Publications,1974), p. 55.

2. J. I. Packer, *Keep in Step with the Spirit* (Old Tappan: Fleming H. Revell Company, 1984), p. 67.

3. *Ibid.*, p. 66.

4. The preposition περὶ, translated 'concerning' or 'about', emphasizes content.

5. 'We do not really know God until he speaks and acts, and he has done so decisively and definitively in the history mirrored in Holy Scripture, culminating in Jesus Christ – the center and goal of Scripture.' Donald G. Bloesch, *God The Almighty* (Downers Grove: InterVarsity Press, 1995), pp. 74-75.

6. See Brian Chapell, *Christ-Centered Preaching* (Grand Rapids: Baker Book House, 1994), Edmund Clowney, *The Unfolding Mystery: Discovering Christ in the Old Testament* (Phillipsburg: Presbyterian and Reformed Publishing Company, 1988), and Sidney Greidanus, *The Modern Preacher and the Ancient Text* (Grand Rapids: William Eerdmans Publishing Company, 1988), *et al.*

7. Michael Horton, 'Repentance, Recovery, and Confession', *The Formal Papers of The Alliance of Confessing Evangelicals' Summit* (April 17-20, 1996), pp. 17-18.

8. John Calvin, *The Gospel According to St. John* (rep. ed., Grand Rapids: William Eerdmans Publishing Company, 1974), vol. 2, p. 139.

9. Charles Haddon Spurgeon, 'Christ Precious to Believers', *The New Park Street Pulpit* (London: Passmore and Alabaster, 1860), p. 140.

10. '*Into all truth* is misleading, for it can be taken to imply that the Church will be guided by the Spirit into the truth about all subjects....The Greek means 'all *the* truth,' i.e., the specific truth about the Person of Jesus and the significance of what He said and did. The existence of the New Testament is permanent evidence that the apostles were guided into truth about this.' R.V.G. Tasker, *The Gospel According to St. John* (Grand Rapids: William B. Eerdmans Publishing Company, 1960), p. 181.

11. To be sure, a *realized* eschatology tends to be the emphasis of the fourth Gospel. However, John does not omit distinct reference to the future

(cf. 5:28-29; 6:39-40; 14:1-3). Most commentators agree that future consummation must not be ruled out here. '... *what is yet to come* refers to all that transpires *in consequence* of the pivotal revelation bound up with Jesus' person, ministry, death, resurrection, and exaltation. This includes ... the pattern of life and obedience under the inbreaking kingdom, up to and including the consummation.' D. A. Carson, *The Gospel According to John* (Grand Rapids: William B. Eerdmans Publishing Company, 1991), p. 540. See also J. H. Bernard, *A Critical and Exegetical Commentary on the Gospel According to St. John* (Edinburgh: T & T Clark, 1985), vol. 2, p. 511.

12. J. Theodore Mueller, 'The Holy Spirit and the Scriptures', *Revelation and the Bible,* ed. Carl F. H. Henry (Grand Rapids: Baker Book House, 1958), p. 269.

13. Bernard Ramm, *After Fundamentalism* (San Francisco: Harper and Row Publishers, 1983), p. 80.

14. Borrowing an illustrative concept from Brian Chapell, Bible expositors need to employ two kinds of lenses when reading the scriptures. We need to employ an exegetical magnifying glass to examine the details of a passage with close scrutiny. We also need to employ a theological fish-eye lens to see how a particular passage fits into the overall redemptive emphasis of the Bible. Chapell, *Christ-Centered Preaching,* p. 269.

15. John Owen, *The Works of John Owen* (repr. ed., Carlisle: The Banner of Truth Trust, 1981), vol. 3, p. 196.

16. John Jennings, 'Of Preaching Christ', *The Christian Pastor's Manual,* ed. John Brown (repr. ed., Pittsburgh: Soli Deo Gloria Publications, 1991), p. 39.

17. William Still, 'The Holy Spirit in Preaching', *Christianity Today* (Sept. 2, 1957), p. 8.

18. Edmund P. Clowney, 'Preaching Christ from all the Scriptures', *The Preacher and Preaching,* ed. Samuel T. Logan (Phillipsburg: Presbyterian and Reformed Publishing Company, 1986), p. 165.

19. Charles Haddon Spurgeon, *The Greatest Fight in the World* (Sovereign Grace Book Club, n.d.), pp. 37, 39.

4

THE EVANGELICAL PRIORITY

The excellency of a sermon lies in the plainest discoveries and
liveliest applications of Jesus Christ.
JOHN FLAVEL

Let Christ be the diamond to shine in the bosom of all your sermons.
BISHOP REYNOLDS

The two points that determine whether a sermon is in accord with
revelation are Christmas and the day of Christ.
KARL BARTH

The Great Paradox

I have attempted, thus far, to establish the component parts of
biblical truth that, when brought together, comprise the doctrine
referred to as 'the the vitality of the Holy Spirit'. As a consequence
of the redemptive mission of Jesus Christ, God's new covenant
promise would be given to His people: the indwelling Holy
Spirit. According to His power, believers would accomplish the
'greater works', which are the advancement of the gospel. What
is the primary ministry of the coming Holy Spirit? To reveal and
glorify Jesus Christ through the communication of divine truth:
objectively, through the means of the inscripturated,
Christocentric word; and, subjectively, through the means of
illuminating these same scriptures to the human heart. How is
this word to be made known? Through the proclamation of the
gospel by men, clothed with an alien power to overcome the
most violent resistance of sinners. Summarized, we defined it as
follows: *the vitality of the Spirit is His effectual work of*

glorifying Jesus Christ through fallible men who faithfully proclaim the Christocentric scriptures. This is ministry distinctive to the new covenant people of God. Jesus Christ is the divinely-delivered message. Proclaiming Him from all of the scriptures is the divinely-ordained method. The attending power of the purchased Holy Spirit is the divinely-appointed means.

The groundwork for this ministry of the Spirit has been established from the Gospels; more particularly, from the words of Jesus Himself. It is interesting to note, however, that as one moves further into the New Testament he can discover that the practice of apostolic ministry was thoroughly consistent with the instruction of Jesus, specifically as it relates to message, method, and means. Several passages make this evident, and none is more obvious than 1 Corinthians 2:1-5. It is to this text we now turn our attention.

Of Paul's many epistles, the two which have been preserved as 1 and 2 Corinthians are filled with various kinds of Christian paradox; statements which seem self-contradictory.[1] For example, in 1 Corinthians 7:29 Paul exhorts married men to live as though they had no wives. Such a statement appears contradictory. In 2 Corinthians Paul talks about poor men who make others rich, those who possess nothing but simultaneously possess all things, being sorrowful but always rejoicing, being unknown and well-known, dying yet living. In chapter 12 he strangely speaks of strength perfected in weakness, a paradox to which we will give some consideration in a future chapter. Many paradoxical statements are woven throughout the fabric of the two Corinthian letters. But each of these grows out of the great paradox that appears in the opening chapter of the first epistle; namely, the paradox of the gospel itself, the seemingly contradictory fact that a weak and foolish message contains the power and wisdom of God Himself.

Paul addresses this concern, at least in part, because the triumphalistic Corinthians had apparently grown ashamed of the gospel. To be sure, they were susceptible to the prevailing attitudes of their day. Buzzing around them were disparaging spirits: 'A crucified Savior? What a powerless gospel.' 'A cross-kind of message? How utterly foolish.' To the contrary, the advocacy of the culture was as follows: 'Power prevails. Wisdom impresses.' Paul, therefore, aims directly at this Corinthian vulnerability and says, in effect, 'Here is a paradox, my dear Corinthian brothers: the things that seem weak and foolish to the world around you are the very things that display the glory of our God; in particular, His power and wisdom.' Moreover, to establish this point, Paul then draws upon three lines of evidence set forth in three subsequent paragraphs:

(1) *God's power and wisdom are displayed in the weak and foolish message that provides salvation for those who believe* (1 Cor. 1:18-25). 'Do not be ashamed of things that appear weak and foolish in the estimation of the world. It was this apparently weak and foolish message that saved you';

(2) *God's power and wisdom are displayed in the weak and foolish people He has determined to save* (1 Cor. 1:26-31). 'Lest you forget, you were not saved because of your significance and value as human beings. The fact is, your own obvious weakness and unworthiness magnified the power and wisdom of God'; and,

(3) *God's power and wisdom are displayed in the weak and foolish ministers who attempt to accomplish His work* (1 Cor. 2:1-5). 'Do you remember the nature of my presence among you? There was nothing impressive about me. That, however, was my intention from the outset. I wanted your faith in Jesus Christ to be drawn out by nothing other than the power of God.'

In these three paragraphs Paul seeks to persuade the Corinthians of the paradoxical nature of the gospel; namely, the very things which appear weak and foolish to the world are the means by which God's glory is displayed most powerfully. More narrowly, in the five verses of the third paragraph, Paul surprisingly echoes the same concerns set forth by Jesus in Luke 24. Stated a bit differently, Paul's burden in 1 Corinthians 2:1-5 is to show that apostolic ministry is characterized by a determination to:

(1) proclaim a foolish message; (2) appropriate a foolish method; and, (3) rest upon a foolish means. For the remainder of this chapter we will develop the first of these three principles; namely, *that an apostolic ministry is characterized by a determination to proclaim a foolish message.*

God's Own Testimony

A brief reading of these three paragraphs reveals Paul's repeated reference to the foolishness of his message:

> 'For the word of the cross is to those who are perishing *foolishness...* ' (1 Cor. 1:18).

> '... God was well-pleased through the *foolishness* of the message preached ...' (1 Cor. 1:21).

> '... we preach Christ crucified ... to Gentiles *foolishness*' (1 Cor. 1:23).

Paul's emphasis precipitates an obvious question: why would anyone seek to be a proclaimer of a message so universally regarded as foolish? Though never justifiable, one can understand the powerful temptation to compromise such a message. No minister seeks to be considered unsophisticated and uninformed. Why, then, would any man attempt to preach a message so utterly disregarded by the world? The answer given by Paul grows out of a recognition of the origination of this message: 'And when I came to you, brethren, I did not come with superiority of speech or of wisdom, proclaiming to you *the testimony of God*' (1 Cor. 2:1).[2] This is Paul's initial definition of his preaching content: not his own testimony about God, rather that the testimony he brought to them was *God's own testimony.*[3] This message was not a manifestation of the creative genius of a man, nor the collective wisdom of a group of first-century mystics or philosophers. It was not the offspring of reason. It was the gift of revelation. It was a message that originated with God. For this reason Paul could say elsewhere: 'Let a man regard us in this manner ... stewards of the mysteries of God' (1 Cor. 4:1). In the same vein he later exhorts Timothy: 'Guard ... the treasure which has been entrusted to you' (2 Tim. 1:14). A recognition of its 'givenness' is the reason Paul refused to compromise this 'foolish' message; the conviction that this was God's own testimony.

Paul, then, describes the substance of God's testimony in fuller detail: 'For I determined to know nothing among you except Jesus Christ, and Him crucified' (1 Cor. 2:2). In the previous chapter Paul similarly defines this message as 'the word of the cross' (1 Cor. 1:18), and 'Christ crucified' (1 Cor. 1:23). At this point it should be acknowledged that the content emphasized in Paul's apostolic approach was in no way unique to the Corinthian context, a deviation from his ordinary design. His typical methodology was to proclaim the gospel of Jesus Christ. Some, however, have suggested that prior to his coming to Corinth Paul experimented with a novel approach in Athens (cf. Acts 17–18). Since his preaching was met with little success, however, he returned to his former resolution to preach Christ with simplicity and clarity before coming to Corinth. Such an interpretation is untenable for three obvious reasons:

(1) it ignores the broad emphasis of the book of Acts which seeks to show Paul's pattern of preaching Christ in all circumstances;

(2) it reveals a blindsidedness to the immediate context of Acts 17 which records Paul's preaching of Jesus and the resurrection (Acts 17:18); and,

(3) it fails to acknowledge that people were saved under the preaching of Paul at Mars Hill (Acts 17:34).When Paul asserts 'I determined to know nothing among you ...' he is not referring to a radical breach with a novel ministry methodology tampered with in Athens. If any contrast is to be discerned it is with reference to the Greek philosophers and orators, so prominently prized in Corinth, who were continuously advancing their own speculations. Paul's message, the message from which he never deviated, originated with God and centered on Jesus Christ.

The Tyranny of the Gospel

Faithfulness to the apostolic pattern demands that the substance of Christian preaching be vitally connected to Jesus Christ and His redemptive accomplishments. This does not imply that our preaching needs to be evangelistic in order to be Christian. It does mean that to be Christian our preaching needs to be evangelical. It means that we cannot divorce the gospel from the rest of the Bible; rather that the Bible now comes to us through the grid of the gospel. The sharp dichotomy between the kerygmatic and didactic, made popular by the British theologian C. H. Dodd,[4] seems spurious. His influence, nevertheless, has been pervasive. Consequently, among preachers of this generation, two tragic assumptions have ensued: (1) the proclamation of the gospel is not properly suited to a Christian context; and (2) anything of a doctrinal nature is altogether inappropriate for a setting of unbelievers. This is a disjunction, however, that the Bible does not make.[5] Such rigid, ironclad categories are foreign to New Testament revelation, and ultimately devastating to the people of God because they inevitably lead to moralism. All of our preaching, including the preaching and teaching of ethical and moral demands, needs to be vitally connected to Jesus Christ and grounded in the consummate act of redemptive history. This is the evangelical priority for all Christian preaching. It is at this point that evangelicals would do well to listen to Karl Barth, who tells us that preaching is truly Christian when it falls within the boundaries of Christmas and the day of Christ.[6] By this Barth is not suggesting that Christian preaching can only occur from the New Testament. Rather, he is saying that we cannot preach from the Old Testament as though the incarnation of God in Christ never took place. To do so would be akin to teaching American history apart from the significance of 1492, 1776, or 1865.[7] Donald Coggan states:

> The Christian preacher has a boundary set for him. When he enters the pulpit, he is not an entirely free man. There is a very real sense in which it may be said of him that the Almighty has set him his

bounds that he shall not pass. He is not at liberty to invent or choose his message: it has been committed to him, and it is for him to declare, expound and commend it to his hearers .... It is a great thing to come under the magnificent tyranny of the gospel.[8]

Another adds:

True Christian preaching must center on the cross of Jesus Christ. The cross is the central doctrine of the holy scriptures. All other revealed truths either find their fulfillment in the cross or are necessarily founded upon it. Therefore, no doctrine of scripture may faithfully be set before men unless it is displayed in its relationship to the cross. The one who is called to preach, therefore, must preach Christ because there is no other message from God.[9]

Why is it that 'Jesus Christ, and Him crucified' should be the nucleus of all Christian preaching? Consider the following three reasons:

(1) *Our primary objective is the salvation of sinners.* Hence, says Bridges:

We are not to commence with the outskirts of the gospel, and so reason on step by step till we come to Christ – thus keeping the sinner waiting in the dark. He wants to see the king. There needs no long ceremonial of approach from a distance. Let the great object be placed in immediate view. Every thing short of this is a grand impertinence. The sinner is dying, he is in instant, urgent, need of the physician and the remedy. The brazen serpent must be lifted up before him – *not because he believes: but because he needs, and that he may believe.*[10]

If such is our primary concern, the following passages compel us to preach a Christocentric message: '.. there is no other name under heaven that has been given among men, by which we must be saved' (Acts 4:12). '... no one comes to the Father, but through Me' (John 14:6). '... the word of the cross ... to us who are being saved it is the power of God' (1 Cor. 1:18);

(2) *Jesus Christ is the focal-point of all biblical revelation.* We have not been faithful to the Spirit-intended purpose of a

particular text if in rightly exegeting its parts we neglect to see its place in the overall redemptive thrust of the Bible. Bridges warns of the consequences of this neglect:

> Many important truths of the gospel may be preached in a disjointed manner; and yet the gospel itself, truly speaking, not be preached. The perfections of God, without a view of their harmony in the work of Christ – the purposes of God, unconnected with the freeness and holiness of the gospel – the glories of heaven, without a reference to Christ as the way thither – the power, defilement, guilt, and condemnation of sin, separated from the doctrine of salvation through Christ – the work of the Holy Spirit, unconnected with the doctrine of the atonement – holiness irrespective of union with Christ—his imputed righteousness disunited from his imparted righteousness – the reception of him by faith, without its active working in the renewal of the heart – the exhibition of promises, separated from duties; or of the duties, independent of their constraining motives – these may be severally portions of the gospel; but, being broken off from their Scriptural connexion, they do not constitute the preaching of the gospel. These broken fragments of truth cannot produce that solid foundation and superstructure of Christian doctrine, by which the temple of God is raised. Misplacing of the truths of the gospel, like confusion in the machinery of clock-work, makes the whole system go wrong.[11]

As a practical model, Packer commends the Puritans:

> Puritan preaching revolved around 'Christ, and him crucified'– for this is the hub of the Bible. The preachers' commission is to declare the whole counsel of God; but the cross is the centre of that counsel, and the Puritans knew that the traveller through the Bible landscape misses his way as soon as he loses sight of the hill called Calvary.[12]

Finally, Jay Adams exhorts: 'Preach Christ in all the scriptures: He is the subject matter of the whole Bible. He is there. Until you have found Him in your preaching portion, you are not ready to preach'[13]; and,

3) Preaching the gospel has been commanded by Jesus Christ and modeled by apostolic practice. 'Go into all the world and preach the gospel to all creation' (Mark 16:15). '... you shall be My witnesses' (Acts 1:8). By clear command of the resurrected Lord, apostolic preaching should be preoccupied with Him. Moreover, the record of New Testament scripture steadily reveals the faithfulness of the apostolic community to the evangelical priority:

> And every day, in the temple and from house to house, they kept right on *teaching and preaching Jesus as the Christ* (Acts 5:42).

> And Philip went down to the city of Samaria and began *proclaiming Christ* to them (Acts 8:5).

> And Philip opened his mouth, and beginning from this scripture he *preached Jesus* to him (Acts 8:35).

> ... and immediately he began to *proclaim Jesus* in the synagogues, saying, 'He is the Son of God' (Acts 9:20).

> But there were some of them, men of Cyprus and Cyrene, who came to Antioch and began speaking to the Greeks also, *preaching the Lord Jesus* (Acts 11:20).

> ... according to Paul's custom, he went to them ... explaining and giving evidence that the Christ had to suffer and rise again from the dead, and saying, *'This Jesus whom I am proclaiming to you is the Christ'* (Acts 17:2-3).

> For Christ did not send me to baptize, but to *preach the gospel...* (1 Cor. 1:17).

> ... but we *preach Christ crucified* (1 Cor. 1:23).

> For we do not *preach* ourselves but *Christ Jesus as Lord* (2 Cor. 4:5).

> You foolish Galatians, who has bewitched you, before whose eyes *Jesus Christ was publicly portrayed as crucified?* (Gal. 3:1).

> To me, the very least of all saints, this grace was given, *to preach to the Gentiles the unfathomable riches of Christ* (Eph. 3:8).

Some may counter at this point, 'Most, if not all, of the aforementioned passages speak to an evangelistic context. In these kinds of settings it is appropriate to preach Christ.' But give consideration to Paul's Corinthian ministry. Acts 18 indicates that the duration of Paul's efforts in Corinth amounted to eighteen months. Certainly his stay could not be defined as a short-term evangelistic crusade. Moreover, after Silas and Timothy arrived from Macedonia, Paul began 'devoting himself completely to the word ... teaching the word of God among them' (Acts 18:5, 11). How was it, then, that for eighteen months Paul preached nothing except '...Jesus Christ, and Him crucified?' Consider the breadth of content contained in this phrase. The name 'Jesus' carries implications related to His personhood; including, it would seem, the mysteries attached to the incarnation. The title 'Christ' recognizes His office as Messianic King; addressing, among other things, the fulfillment of several Old Testament promises. The perfect participle 'crucified' has reference to His redemptive accomplishments and their attendant consequences. May I suggest that eighteen months is not time enough to plumb the depths of the person, office, and work of the Son of God? Eighteen years would prove insufficient for such a task.

'But,' someone may ask, 'is there a place for preaching the ethical commands of the Bible? Is there a place for speaking to husbands and wives? Is there a place for establishing a Christian work ethic? Is there a place for challenging our children toward certain moral behaviors?' And we resoundingly respond in the affirmative. But we must never preach them in a way that would be suitable in a Jewish synagogue, an Islamic mosque, or a Mormon temple. If our message is appropriate to settings such as these we are not preaching a Christian message. A preacher, for example, may proclaim to an irresponsible husband, 'You should love your wife in a selfless manner.' At this point, however, he has yet to say anything distinctly Christian. Just as easily could this message have come from John Bradshaw, Harold Kushner, or Louis Farakan. Christian preaching, on the other hand, grounds the ethical imperatives in redemptive indicatives. 'You have a command, dear brother. You must love your wife selflessly. To be sure, this is an awesome task. But consider the following: the *source* of this command is the Lord Jesus Christ, the *model* of this command is observed in His own great sacrifice, the *strength* for this command lies in His purchase of the Holy Spirit, and finally, if disregarded, the encouragement to *resume* this command is found in the forgiveness He offers because of His work of redemption.' Chapell further illustrates:

> Unless we identify the redemptive purposes in a text it is possible to say all the right words and yet send all the wrong signals. I witness this miscommunication almost daily on the top-rated radio station in our city that broadcasts a morning 'meditation'. Each morning the preacher addresses some topic with a Bible verse or two. The subjects run the gamut from procrastination, to parenting, to honesty on the job. The station turns up the reverberation whenever this preacher speaks so that it sounds as though the words come direct from Mount Sinai. Not to pay attention seems like a sin. I would guess that few even question the content of the man's words. As he reminds us from the Bible to practice punctuality, good parenting, and business propriety, I realize a hundred thousand motorists are nodding their heads and saying in unison, 'That's right ... that's how we should live.'
>
> I have even played tapes of this preacher's meditations to seminary classes and asked if anyone can discern error in what he says. Rarely does anyone spot a problem. The preacher quotes his text accurately, he advocates moral causes, and he encourages loving behaviors. The problem that I point out to students and that is carefully hidden from the broadcast audience is that the radio preacher is not a Christian. He represents a large cult headquartered in our region.
>
> How can this be? How can so many Christians (even those well-informed) so readily grant assent to one whose communications are radically anti-Christian? Some answer that their lack of protest results from the radio preacher's care to avoid saying anything controversial. They contend that he hides his heresy beneath a veil of right-sounding orthodoxy. Such defenses miss the point even as his proponents have missed the problem. The radio preacher has

not hidden his heresy; he exposes it every time he speaks in what he fails to say. The real problem is that evangelical preachers inadvertently and so frequently present such similar messages that Christians fail to hear the difference between a message that purports to be biblical and one that actually is.

A message that merely advocates morality and compassion remains sub-Christian even if the preacher can prove that the Bible demands such behaviors.[14]

An apostolic ministry is resolutely determined to proclaim a foolish message: 'the gospel ... the word of the cross ... Christ crucified ... the testimony of God ... Jesus Christ, and Him crucified' (1 Cor. 1:17-18, 23; 2:1-2). The evangelical priority is the regulative principle for all Christian preaching. But why must this be true? Because of the great paradox: the power of God in the weak and foolish thing. 'For the word of the cross is to those who are perishing foolishness, *but to us who are being saved it is the power of God'* (1 Cor. 1:18).

Preach Christ Jesus the Lord. Determine to nothing among your people, but Christ crucified. Let his name and grace, his spirit and love, triumph in the midst of all your sermons. Let your great end be, to glorify him in the heart, to render him amiable and precious in the eyes of his people, to lead them to him, as a sanctuary to protect them, a propitiation to reconcile them, a treasure to enrich them, a physician to heal them, an advocate to present them and their services to God, as wisdom to counsel them, as righteousness to justify, as sanctification to renew, as redemption to save. Let Christ *be the diamond to shine in the bosom of all your sermons.*[15]

Notes

1. C. K. Barrett, *The First Epistle to the Corinthians* (Peabody: Hendrickson Publishers, 1968), p. 64.

2. Some manuscripts read τὸ μυστήριον τοῦ θεοῦ, 'the mystery of God'. The difference is very slight and is of no real significance in terms of the intended point.

3. This is best understood as a subjective genitive; *i.e.,* the noun in the genitive (θεοῦ) acts as the subject of, or does the action implied in the noun to which it stands related (μαρτύριον).

4. 'The New Testament writers draw a clear distinction between preaching and teaching .... Teaching (*didaskein*) is in a large majority of cases ethical instruction.... Preaching, on the other hand, is public proclamation of Christianity to the non-Christian world .... For the early Church, then, to preach the gospel was by no means the same thing as to deliver moral instruction or exhortation.' C.H. Dodd, *Apostolic Preaching and its Developments* (New York: Harper & Row Publishers, 1964), pp. 7, 8.

5. 'Matthew relates that Jesus was 'teaching (*didaskon*) in their synagogues and preaching (*kerysson*) the gospel of the kingdom' (4:23; cf. 9:35; 11:1). Luke similarly reports that Jesus 'taught (*edidasken*) in their synagogues' and a little later that Jesus was engaged in 'preaching (*kerysson*) in the synagogues' (4:15, 44). In Rome Paul was engaged in 'preaching (*kerysson*) the kingdom of God and teaching (*didaskon*) about the the Lord Jesus Christ' (Acts 28:31). Thus, in one and the same place, both kinds of activity went on: teaching and proclaiming. Although preaching in a mission situation must have had a different emphasis than preaching in an established church, there appears to be a developing consensus today that "preaching and teaching were never sharply separated by the first Christians and should not be separated by us today".' Sidney Greidanus, *The Modern Preacher and the Ancient Text* (Grand Rapids: William B. Eerdmans Publishing Company, 1988), p. 7, referring to R. C. Worley, *Preaching and Teaching in the Earliest Church* (Philadelphia: Westminster Press, 1967).

6. Karl Barth, *Homiletics* (Louisville: John Knox Press, 1991), p. 55.

7. This parallel has been borrowed from two lectures delivered by Thomas N. Smith, 'The Preaching that is Christian: Keeping the Supreme and Central Thing Supreme and Central' (Cordelia: The Whitefield Ministerial Fraternal), Nov. 4, 1996.

8. Donald F. Coggan, *Stewards of Grace* (London: Hodder & Stoughton, 1958), pp. 46, 48.

9. Thomas F. Jones, 'Preaching the Cross of Christ', an unpublished essay presented in 1976-1977 homiletics lectures at Covenant Theological Seminary, p. 1. Cited in Brian Chapell, *Christ-Centered Preaching* (Grand Rapids: Baker Book House, 1994), p. 271.

10. Charles Bridges, *The Christian Ministry* (repr. ed., Carlisle: The

Banner of Truth Trust, 1991), p. 252.

   11. *Ibid.*, pp. 253-254.

   12. J. I. Packer, *A Quest for Godliness* (Wheaton: Crossway Books, 1990), p. 286.

   13. Jay E. Adams, *Preaching with Purpose* (Grand Rapids: Zondervan Publishing House, 1982), p. 152.

   14. Chapell, *Preaching,* pp. 267-268.

   15. Bishop Reynolds, *Works,* pp. 1039-1040. Cited in Bridges, *Ministry,* p. 258.

5

THE DECISIVE FUNCTION OF THE CHURCH

It was by the ear, by our first parents listening to the
serpent that we lost paradise; and it is by the ear,
by hearing of the word, that we get to heaven.
THOMAS WATSON

The public ministry of the word is the most responsible part
of our work – the grand momentum of Divine agency –
the most extensive engine of Ministerial operation.
CHARLES BRIDGES

Preaching is God's own word. That is to say,
through the activity of preaching, God himself speaks.
KARL BARTH

Is Methodology Neutral?

In May of 1991 an article appeared in *The Wall Street Journal*
entitled, "Mighty Fortresses: Megachurches Strive to be all
Things to all Parishioners." The article documents some of the
novel methods currently employed by local churches to boost
attendance and lure the unsaved in their communities. One
example cited was that of a staged wrestling match sponsored by
a local church and featuring church employees. The purpose for
this event was to initiate greater participation for Sunday evening
services. The writer of the article notes some of the necessary
preparations involved: 'To train for the event, 10 game
employees got lessons from Tugboat Taylor, a former professional
wrestler, in pulling hair, kicking shins and tossing bodies around
without doing real harm.'[1] In an earlier, but similar, article it

was reported that a half-million dollar special-effects system, designed to produce smoke, fire, sparks, and laser lights, had recently been installed in the auditorium of a large southwestern church. Various staff members were sent to Bally's Casino in Las Vegas to acquire the necessary skills to perform live special effects. Sometime later, the pastor of this church concluded a sermon by ascending to 'heaven' via invisible wires that drew him up out of sight while the choir and orchestra added musical accompaniment to the smoke, fire, and light show.[2] About this pastor the article boasts:

> He packs his church with such special effects as ... cranking up a chain saw and toppling a tree to make a point ... the biggest Fourth of July fireworks display in town and a Christmas service with a rented elephant, kangaroo and zebra. The Christmas show features 100 clowns with gifts for the congregation's children.[3]

Surprisingly, these are not obscure citations from eccentric congregations. They are common occurrences in churches which are regarded as evangelically mainstream. Similar examples could be drawn from many of the most widely-recognized churches across the United States. The novelty of these 'ministry methodologies', however, along with their increasing receptivity and growing prominence, necessitate some discriminating consideration on the part of clear-thinking evangelicals. How are these methods of gospel ministry to be regarded? Do the scriptures affirm that 'anything goes' in the name of reaching people for Jesus Christ? Is it true, as is often stipulated, that ministry methods are of no significance to God insofar as the message of the gospel is clearly communicated? Is it accurate to conclude that style by itself is neither good nor bad, but always neutral?

Recently, I came across a brochure that was being displayed at a local coffee shop. It had been placed there for the purpose of inviting people to a nearby church. On the cover of this brochure was a man, the pastor of the church, dressed in a bunny suit, wearing a pair of designer sun glasses. Dejectedly, he sits on a marching-band bass drum. The caption under this picture made an obvious connection to a series of television commercials which advertise a well-known brand of batteries. It read as follows:

'When the Power Bunny runs out of energy to keep going, going, going ...
(open to the inside of this brochure) ...
the Easter message can give you the power for living, living, living!
Nothing outlasts the resurrection power of Jesus Christ!'

Beneath this caption is a second picture of the pastor in a bunny suit, but now in an altogether different light. He is smiling from ear to ear, bass drum strapped to his shoulders, now marching with vigor and enthusiasm as a consequence of his newly-discovered energy. A quote then follows:

"I came so that you can have real and eternal life,
more and better life than you ever dreamed of."
Jesus (John 10:10).

Of all that I have ever seen in the name of Christian marketing, this was clearly the most distasteful. 'But why?' I wondered. For several days I posed to myself the question, 'What is it about that brochure that disturbs me so deeply?' The answer became apparent from the passage to which we have recently turned our attention. Stated simply, from the perspective of the Apostle Paul, style is not neutral. When the gospel is the message, the methodology of its presentation is not irrelevant. Paul's concern in 1 Corinthians 2 is to make evident that the cross of Jesus Christ not only establishes the *substance* of our preaching, it determines the *style* in which we communicate it. In other words, message and method must be harmonious. When they are not, it is the integrity of the message that suffers.

Before proceeding any further, it is essential that we alert ourselves to the possibility of losing focus on the issue of concern. It must be acknowledged that our reservation concerning many of these novel ministry methodologies has nothing to do with preferring a traditional style of ministry over against a more contemporary emphasis. Contemporaneity is not the issue. Effectual Christianity will always prove contemporary to the unique mission-field given to it by Jesus Christ. Rather, the issue in view is *the radical inconsistency that exists between the message of a bloody cross and the slick, sophisticated, Spielberg-like methods of communicating it.* Paul's burden is to assert that true, apostolic ministry is characterized by an intimate correspondence of message and method; that thorough-going consistency is to exist between the word of the cross and its articulation. The great violinist, Yehudi Menuhin, was asked on one occasion to define the secret of his genius. He offered a one-word answer: surrender. The violinist must surrender to the violin.[4] In much the same way, the preacher must surrender to the lordship of the gospel. It must reign supreme. Its message must be so deeply incarnated into the man of God that not only will it permeate everything he says, its very scent will be evident in his manner of communicating it. Thus, it is evident that an apostolic ministry is characterized, not only by a determination to proclaim a foolish message, *but a determination to appropriate a foolish method.*

Recovering The Priority

Has God ordained a method for making known the message of the cross? Or, is methodology something that can be shaped by the unique cultural mores of each generation? Paul appears resoundingly consistent in the context of 1 Corinthians 1–2:

> For Christ did not send me to baptize, but to *preach* the gospel... (1 Cor. 1:17).

> ... God was well-pleased through the foolishness of the message *preached* to save those who believe (1 Cor. 1:21).

> ... but we *preach* Christ crucified ... (1 Cor. 1:23).

> And when I came ... *proclaiming* to you the testimony of God (1 Cor. 2:1).

And my message and my *preaching* were not in persuasive words
of wisdom ... (1 Cor. 2:4).

A brief examination of a Bible concordance reveals that the
English words 'preach', 'preaching', 'proclaim' and 'proclaiming' are used over one hundred times in the New Testament
scriptures. Greidanus states that the New Testament employs as
many as thirty-three different verbs to describe what we usually
cover with the single word 'preaching'.[5]

Despite the frequency with which the scriptures refer to
preaching, many contemporary evangelicals seem astonished by
this emphasis. Some even appear to take tacit offense at this
assertion of biblical truth.[6] Unfortunately, in the much-needed
recovery of an 'every-member ministry', evangelicals have
correspondingly misplaced the priority recovered by their
forebears in the Reformation; namely, the centrality of preaching.[7]
Some in pastoral ministry have failed to recognize the emphasis
of biblical revelation which steadily establishes preaching as
the primary method of communicating the message of the gospel.

As a corrective, one should give consideration to the terms
by which Jesus defined His ministry:

'The Spirit of the Lord is upon Me, because He anointed Me to
preach the gospel to the poor. He has sent Me to *proclaim* release
to the captives, and recovery of sight to the blind, to set free those
who are downtrodden, to *proclaim* the favorable year of the Lord'
(Luke 4:18-19).

It is not surprising, then, that following His baptism, Matthew
records: 'Jesus began to *preach*' (Matt. 4:17). The Gospel of
Mark sheds further light on this priority of Jesus: 'Let us go somewhere else to the towns nearby, in order that I may *preach* there
also; for that is what I came out for' (Mark 1:38). Two chapters
later Mark records Jesus' rationale for choosing His disciples:
'And He appointed twelve, that they might be with Him, and that
He might send them out to *preach*' (Mark 3:14). Moreover, this
design was to continue following His resurrection: 'Go into all

the world and *preach* the gospel to all creation' (Mark 16:15). This commission was thoroughly embraced by the disciples, and especially Peter, as is made evident in the book of Acts. About this divinely-appointed methodology Peter says to Cornelius: 'And He ordered us to *preach* to the people' (Acts 10:42).

Paul's conviction about preaching was equally resolute. He explains to the Jews in Antioch: 'And we *preach* to you the good news of the promise made to the fathers' (Acts 13:32). In his letter to the Romans Paul reveals something of his desire for ministry with the Christians in Rome: 'Thus, for my part, I am eager to *preach* the gospel to you also ...' (Rom. 1:15). This verse, in particular, is of noteworthy interest, given the fact that Paul desires to preach the gospel to *Christians* (cf. Rom. 1:7). Later, he writes more specifically concerning God's saving design through preaching:

> Whoever will call upon the name of the Lord will be saved. How then shall they call upon Him in whom they have not believed? And how shall they believe in Him whom they have not heard? And how shall they hear without a *preacher*? (Rom. 10:13-14).

In 1 Corinthians 9 Paul exposes the burden of every man appointed by God to this work: 'For if I *preach* the gospel, I have nothing to boast of, for I am under compulsion; for woe is me if I do not *preach* the gospel' (1 Cor. 9:16). So as to verify his rightful place among the apostles Paul says matter-of-factly: 'Whether then it was I or they, so we *preach* and so you believed' (1 Cor. 15:11). Finally, in anticipation of his imminent execution, the great Apostle gives a concluding exhortation to young Timothy: '*preach* the word' (2 Tim. 4:2). In summary, preaching was a prominent feature in the ministry methodology of Jesus, the stated reason for which He was anointed of the Spirit of God. It was the specific work to which He called His disciples, the reason for which they, too, would be clothed with the power of the Spirit (cf. Luke 24:49). Furthermore, they continued the pattern of this methodology by exhorting subsequent disciples to this same task.[8]

How altogether different are the priorities of ministry within contemporary evangelicalism. It is a colossal understatement to suggest that preaching and preachers have fallen on hard times in recent years. Christians themselves often speak of preaching in disparaging tones. Political correctness demands that the man of God no longer be regarded as 'a preacher', but instead, 'a communicator'. An *absence* of preaching is often the means now employed to attract people to the assembly on the Lord's Day. 'Come to our church. Our pastor won't preach at you,' it is promised. Television sit-coms frequently portray preachers as irrelevant and empty-headed buffoons. 'From what do these kinds of attitudes stem?' it should be asked. Some would be quick to suggest the anti-authoritarian mood of our day: 'Most people will welcome a word of encouragement. Some may accept a social commentary of sorts. But few in our day, if any, will tolerate preaching that is authoritative.' While, for the most part, this assessment is accurate, it is not my chief concern. Rather, I am convinced that preaching is held in such low esteem today because a great many preachers are so utterly inept at the task.

To what can this ineptitude be attributed? To be sure, some lack calling and giftedness. Of course, this is no reflection upon the spiritual integrity of such men, nor on the potential of their usefulness to the kingdom of God. It is to say that some men are not suited to pulpit ministry because God in His sovereignty has not appointed them to this particular task. One can remember the scene from the movie *Chariots of Fire* when Harold Abrahams solicits the personal tutelage of a famous track and field coach, Sam Mussabini. Following Abrahams' request, Mussabini replies: 'You see, Mr. Abrahams, like the bridegroom, it's the coach that should do the asking .... we've an old saying in my game, son: you can't put in what God's left out.' The New Testament certainly affirms the priesthood of all believers. It does not, however, espouse a 'preacherhood' of all believers. The experience of regeneration and the presence of the indwelling Spirit, matched with sincere desire, does not fit a man for the ministry of proclamation. Such is the consequence of the sovereign calling and gifting of God.[9]

Some men are inept at preaching because they lack diligence; the pastorate is an effective hiding place for lazy men. Other men lack understanding. That is to say, they have yet to recognize the priority of preaching in God's design. A pastor may find himself overseeing the Sunday School program, directing the children's ministry, leading the men's Bible Study, or readily available for counseling. Consequently, it is not uncommon to hear: 'Pastor Smith is a great guy, and a genuine servant. I'm just not fed by his preaching.' In defense, some would be quick to assert: 'But these other ministries are important.' Certainly this is true. But at this point it must be asked, what kind of priority did the original apostles give to the role of preaching when the need for other ministries became apparent? When the legitimate demands of people threatened the apostles' commitment to the preoccupation assigned to them by Jesus, these needs were addressed by the appointment of a second group of spiritually mature men. Does this delegation reflect laziness on the part of the original apostles? Worse yet, does it betray a sense of spiritual superiority on their parts? No, it is nothing but a division of labor that seeks to protect the centrality of preaching in God's design. 'It is not desirable for us to neglect the word of God in order to serve tables .... we will devote ourselves to prayer, and to the ministry of the word' (Acts 6:2-4).

Preachers (and their congregations!) must understand that faithfulness to God's methodology will, by necessity, exempt them from significant participation in most other ministry responsibilities. When referring to elders worthy of double honor, Paul describes them as men who work to the point of exhaustion[10] at 'preaching and teaching' (1 Tim. 5:17). An assumption should be obvious at this point: if men such as these, given to preaching and teaching, labor unto weariness in this work, then it is highly unlikely they will have significant involvement with other ministries, however important they may be. Faithful exposition is an all-consuming work; a faithful man immovable from this design. He recognizes preaching as the method ordained of God. Marcel states it as succinctly as it can be stated: 'Preaching is the central, primary, decisive function of the Church.'[11] From the historical perspective Lloyd-Jones adds:

> Is it not clear, as you take a bird's-eye view of Church history, that the decadent periods and eras in the history of the Church have always been those periods when preaching had declined? What is it that always heralds the dawn of a Reformation or of a Revival. It is renewed preaching.[12]

A Declaration That Demands Compliance

Why does the New Testament steadily set forth preaching as the principle method of communicating the gospel? Simply stated, it is the method best suited to the nature of the message being made known. The gospel is a message which declares the invasion of God into human history. God has intervened to address the human dilemma by means of His redemptive achievements. Hence, the good news is to be announced. It is to be proclaimed. God is not negotiating with this message. He is not asking for discussion or attempting to strike a bargain. As the Lord of the universe He is declaring a word that demands compliance from His creation. A brief consideration of the words used in 1 Corinthians 1– 2 reveals this emphasis.[13] The spirit of the gospel demands a method of communication that is authoritative: 'God has acted. God has come. You must respond.' Preaching then, in this sense, is not 'the delivery of a learned and edifying or hortatory discourse in well-chosen words and a pleasant voice. It is the declaration of an event,'[14] 'urging acceptance and compliance'.[15]

It must be understood that the preacher does not *share,* he *declares.* It is for this very reason that small group Bible studies can never replace the preaching of the gospel. Preaching is not a little talk. It is not a fireside chat. To substitute sharing and discussion for preaching is to risk the integrity of the gospel itself. When a man stands before the people of God with the Christo-centric word on his lips he must say, as it were, 'Thus saith the Lord,' because through the scriptures God still speaks. This is not arrogance on the part of the preacher. Rather, it is an authoritative passion that grows out of a recognition of the nature of the message he has been sent to proclaim. Carson states: 'It is not arrogant to re-present as forcefully as we can God's gospel; it is simply faithful stewardship.'[16] Stott agrees:

> But we preach ... that is, our task as Christian preachers is not subserviently to answer all the questions which men put to us; nor to attempt to meet all the demands which are made on us; nor hesitatingly to make tentative suggestions to the philosophically minded; but rather to proclaim a message which is dogmatic because it is divine. The preacher's responsibility is proclamation, not discussion. There is too much discussion of the Christian religion today, particularly with unbelievers, as if we were more concerned with men's opinions of Christ than with the honour and glory of Jesus Christ Himself. Are we to cast our Priceless Pearl before swine to let them sniff at Him and trample upon Him at their pleasure? No. We are called to proclaim Christ, not to discuss Him. As we have already seen, we are 'heralds,' charged to publish abroad a message which did not originate with us but with Him who gave it to us to publish.[17]

Preaching is the method that best suits the authoritative declaration of God's accomplishments in Jesus Christ. But greater focus is needed at this juncture. It is not wholly accurate to set forth preaching as God's method, apart from a proper understanding of the manner in which this preaching is to express itself. To be sure, Christian preaching is concerned with content. It is also concerned with the character in which the content is communicated. That is to say, Christian preaching consciously renounces all dependence upon humanly-devised techniques of persuasion. Two features were noticeably absent from Paul's preaching ministry in Corinth: 'superiority of speech' and 'wisdom'. In all likelihood the first phrase refers to the *manner* of communication,[18] while the second refers to the *content*,[19] a reference to philosophical speculations so prominent in Corinth.[20] 'When I came to you I did not offer an exposition of a novel philosophical conception,' Paul affirms. 'For that very reason I

refused to draw upon the oratorical techniques of the rhetorician.'
In verse 4 Paul further describes his preaching: 'not in persuasive
words of wisdom.' The word 'persuasive' appears only here in
the New Testament, though its cognate is used in Colossians 2:4
to speak of persuasion that is intentionally deceitful, 'for the
specious and plausible Gnostic philosophers'.[21] In relationship,
then, to 1 Corinthians 2:4 Robertson states: 'Corinth put a
premium on the veneer of false rhetoric and thin thinking.'[22] Barrett
describes this as 'words directed by worldly wisdom'.[23] This
phrase is not a display of false humility on the part of Paul.
Elsewhere he readily acknowledges his attempt to be persuasive
(cf. 2 Cor. 5:11). Nor is this to suggest that Paul was an ineffective
preacher (cf. Acts 14:12). Rather, Paul is reminding the
Corinthians of his conscious intention to renounce the manipulative
techniques of persuasion that were regularly employed in the
Greek culture. Contrariwise, had his message been the product
of his own mind he might have drawn upon these communicative
techniques.

The Holy Correspondence
Suppose, for example, that a mother and father are burdened to
teach the alphabet to their children. Putting on a purple dinosaur
costume and singing the 'ABC' song is an altogether legitimate
method to employ. Suppose a corporation feels the need to boost
profits in its fast-food chain by increasing hamburger sales.
Donning a jack-in-the-box head is equally legitimate. No
incongruity exists between message and method of communication.
On the other hand, something would be radically inappropriate,
however, were approaches such as these employed by the parents
of JonBonet Ramsey in making their television appeal to find
their daughter's murderer. Why would these be so evidently out
of place? Because there would exist an irreconcilable disparity
between the message and the method of its communication.
   The preacher brings to a fallen humanity the very testimony of
God centered on the redemptive work of Jesus Christ, a work
which by nature shatters all human self-sufficiency. To then

attempt a proclamation of that message in a manner that relies upon methods reflecting the wizardry of men is to eviscerate the gospel of its own content. The cross, implies Paul, not only determines the substance of the preacher's message, it dictates the manner in which preachers communicate it; in a way that rivets the attention of people on the beauties of Jesus Christ rather than on the comparatively paltry gifts of the preacher. This is not to diminish giftedness. This is not to justify indolence. This is not an excuse for a lack of exactness. It is to say that a preacher ought never to preach in a manner that consciously draws attention to himself. The Puritan John Flavel coined an important phrase: 'a crucified style best suits the preachers of a crucified Christ.'[24] Christian preaching demands a holy correspondence between message and method. We must always be asking of ourselves and our ministries: 'Is the method I am employing to communicate the gospel in keeping with the essence of the gospel itself? Is this a cross-kind of communication?' John Piper writes:

> ... the cross is the power of God to crucify the pride of both the preacher and the congregation. In the New Testament the cross is not only a past place of objective substitution; it is also a present place of subjective execution – the execution of my self-reliance and love affair with the praise of men.[25]

Here, then, is the dilemma faced by every man called to the work of preaching: he is a sinful man, burdened by his own ego, pride, and desire to succeed. His temptations are like those of other men. He wants to be regarded. He wants to be esteemed. He wants to be loved. He wants to be heard. And so his inclination is say to himself, 'I better excel at this preaching business. I need more humor. I need a more powerful story. How can I polish my technique so as to wholly impress?' The incongruity at this point, however, is evident. If God has supremely disclosed himself in the cross, and if following Jesus Christ means dying daily, then to adopt a style of ministry that is triumphalistic, designed to impress, and calculated to win acclaim is radically inappropriate.

The ministry of Paul, on the other hand, bears the marks of this holy correspondence. In fact, he openly acknowledges the true state of his condition while in Corinth: 'And I was with you in weakness and in fear and in much trembling' (1 Cor. 2:3). One wonders the impression such an admission would leave on a modern-day pastoral search committee. What was the source of Paul's timidity? Among other things, the immensity of the work (trafficking in the eternal souls of men), the inadequacy of his abilities (though brilliant he could not overcome a heart enslaved to sin), and the unthinkable outcome that would result if God did not choose to attend his efforts with power. Hence, Paul's weakness was evident. Piper is right when he says that all genuine preaching is rooted in a feeling of desperation. The preacher wakes up on the Lord's Day morning and he can smell the smoke of hell on one side and feel the crisp breezes of heaven on the other. He then looks down at his pitiful notes and he says to himself, 'Who do I think I am kidding? Is this all there is?'[26] Though oftentimes a source of great anxiety, this is the proper conclusion for the preacher of the cross. He is ever mindful of his inadequacies in relationship to the immensity of the task at hand. Still, he cannot turn away from it. The perspective of Paul steels his nerve: 'For we do not preach ourselves but Christ Jesus as Lord' (2 Cor. 4:5).

Consider the task of John the Baptist: knowingly to prepare the way for someone else. The early days of his ministry were characterized by great enthusiasm, though he always repudiated any Messianic claim. When the public ministry of Jesus finally began, John said to his men, 'Behold, the lamb of God!' (John 1:36). Did John raise his arm and point to Jesus? Did he motion toward Jesus with his head? Did he push his men in the direction of Jesus? About these things the text is silent. But to be sure, the disciples heard the truth in his words: 'And the two disciples heard him speak, and they followed Jesus' (John 1:37). Nowhere is there any indication that they returned to John, even for a visit. Oswald Sanders has captured the ministry of the Baptist in these terms: '... he prepares the way, clears the way, and gets out of the way.'[27] Certainly this is the role of every gospel preacher: to prepare the way, to clear the way, and, when the Son of God comes, to get out of the way. In his journal Robert Murray McCheyne has written the following:

> Today, missed some fine opportunity of speaking a word for Christ. The Lord saw that I would have spoken as much for my honour as for His, and therefore, He shut my mouth. I see that a man cannot be a faithful, fervent minister until he preaches just for Christ's sake, until he gives up trying to attract people to himself, and seeks to attract them to Christ. Lord, give me this.[28]

An apostolic ministry is characterized by a determination to proclaim a foolish message. It is equally devoted to the appropriation of a foolish method. Herein is the holy correspondence for which every Christian preacher should longingly seek.

> When telling Thy salvation free
> Let all absorbing thoughts of Thee
> My heart and soul engross:
> And when all hearts are bowed and stirred
> Beneath the influence of Thy word,
> Hide me behind Thy cross.[29]

Notes
1. R. Gustav Niebuhr, 'Mighty Fortresses: Megachurches Strive to be all Things to all Parishioners', *The Wall Street Journal* (13 May, 1991), sec. A, p. 6.
2. Robert Johnson, 'Heavenly Gifts: Preaching a Gospel of Acquisitiveness, a Showy Sect Prospers', *The Wall Street Journal* (11 December, 1990), sec. A, pp. 1-8.
3. *Ibid.*, sec. A, p. 8.
4. Cited in Tony Sargent, *The Sacred Anointing* (Wheaton: Crossway Books, 1994), p. 121.
5. Sidney Greidanus, *The Modern Preacher and the Ancient Text* (Grand Rapids: William Eerdmans Publishing Company, 1988), p. 6.
6. Contrariwise, evangelicals need to heed the perspective of Bonhoeffer: 'The congregation which is being awakened by the proclamation of the word of God will demonstrate the genuineness of its faith by honouring the office of preaching in its unique glory and by serving it with

all its powers; it will not rely on its own faith or on the universal priesthood of all believers in order to depreciate the office of preaching, to place obstacles in its way, or even to try to make it subordinate to itself', Dietrich Bonhoeffer, *Ethics* (New York: Macmillan Press, 1955), p. 260.

7. 'We are living in an age which is querying about everything, and among these things it is querying the place and the value and the purpose of preaching. In increasing numbers people seem to be depreciating the value of preaching, and they are turning more and more to singing of various types and kinds, accompanied with various kinds of instruments. They are also going back to dramatic representations or recitals of the scripture, and some are going back even to dancing and various other forms of external manifestations of the act of worship. All this is having the effect of depreciating the place and value of preaching .... Now we know that the Reformation – even before you come to the particular Puritan emphasis – swept away all such things. It swept away the medieval 'mystery plays' as they are called, and dramatic performances in the church. The Reformation got rid of all that and it is very sad to observe that people who claim an unusual degree of spirituality should be trying to lead us back to that which the Reformers saw so clearly had been concealing the gospel and the Truth from people. If you mime the scriptures, or give a dramatic representation of them, you are distracting the attention of people from the truth that is conveyed in the scriptures; whereas preaching ... is essentially concerned with bringing out the truth of the Scriptures', D. Martyn Lloyd-Jones, *The Puritans: Their Origins and Successors* (Carlisle: The Banner of Truth Trust, 1987), p. 373.

8. 'Our Lord was a preacher. John the Baptist, the forerunner, was also a preacher primarily. In the Book of Acts we find the same: Peter on the day of Pentecost got up and preached, and he continued to do so. The Apostle Paul was pre-eminently a great preacher. We see him preaching in Athens, as he *declares* the Truth to the Athenians. That was the essential view of preaching held by the Puritans ... and all who believe in the supremacy of preaching have always claimed, that this was our Lord's own method of teaching the Truth', *Ibid.*, pp. 374-375.

9. 'I believe that there should be a place in the church for the exercise of any gift that any individual church member may chance to have; but I am certain that all Christians are not given the gift of expounding the scriptures. All are not called or meant to preach. This is something peculiar and special, and we must get rid of the idea which opposes the preaching of one man who is called to the work...', *Ibid.*, pp. 373-374.

10. The verb, $\kappa o\pi\iota\acute{a}\omega$, means: 'to be tired or weary, as the result of hard or difficult endeavor', Johannes P. Louw and Eugene A. Nida, *Greek-English Lexicon of the New Testament Based on Semantic Domains* (New York: United Bible Societies, 1989), vol. 1, p. 260.

11. Pierre Ch. Marcel, *The Relevance of Preaching* (Grand Rapids: Baker Book House, 1963), p. 18.

12. D. Martyn Lloyd-Jones, *Preaching and Preachers* (Grand Rapids: Zondervan Publishing House, 1971), p. 24.

13. The word 'preach' in 1 Corinthians 1:17 is a translation of εὐαγγελίζω. It means 'to announce good news ... proclaim, to preach', William F. Arndt and F. Wilbur Gingrich, *A Greek-English Lexicon of the New Testament and Other Early Christian Literature* (Chicago: The University of Chicago Press, 1979), p. 317. In 1:23 Paul writes 'we preach Christ'. Here he employs the word κηρύσσω meaning, 'to proclaim aloud, to publicly announce ... an authoritative and public announcement that demands compliance'. C. Brown, 'κηρύσσω', *The New International Dictionary of New Testament Theology*, ed. Colin Brown (Grand Rapids: Zondervan Publishing House, 1979), vol. 3, pp. 44, 48. Paul then speaks of 'proclaiming' God's testimony (1 Cor. 2:1). The word καταγγέλλω means 'to announce, with focus upon the extent to which the announcement or proclamation extends', Louw and Nida, *Semantic Domains,* vol. 1, p. 411. Finally, in 1 Cor. 2:4 Paul refers to his 'preaching'. This term, κήρυγμα, is 'proclamation, preaching ... the phenomena of a call which goes out and makes a claim upon the hearers'. C. Brown, 'κήρυγμα', *DNNT,* vol. 3, p.48, 53.

14. Gerhard Friedrich, 'κηρύσσω', *Theological Dictionary of the New Testament,* ed. Gerhard Kittel (Grand Rapids: William B. Eerdmans Publishing Company, 1965), vol. 3, p. 703.

15. Louw and Nida, *Semantic Domains,* vol. 1, p. 417.

16. D. A. Carson, *The Cross and Christian Ministry: An Exposition of Passages from 1 Corinthians* (Grand Rapids: Baker Book House, 1993), p. 37.

17. John R. W. Stott, *The Preacher's Portrait* (Grand Rapids: William B. Eerdmans Publishing Company, 1961), p. 110.

18. The phrase ὑπεροχὴν λόγου refers to words that are pompous and high sounding. Louw and Nida, *Semantic Domains,* vol. 1, p. 736. Conzelmann renders this: 'Not in such a way as to distinguish myself.' Hans Conzelmann, *1 Corinthians* (Philadelphia: Fortress Press, 1975), p. 53.

19. Gordon D. Fee, *The First Epistle to the Corinthians* (William B. Eerdmans Publishing Company, 1987), pp. 90-91.

20. 'It has been persuasively argued that Paul is alluding to the sophists of his day. Many intellectual movements greatly prized rhetoric. Philosophers were as widely praised for their oratory as for their content. But the sophists brought these ideals to new heights. Following fairly rigid and somewhat artificial conventions, these public speakers were praised and followed (and gained paying students!) in proportion to their ability to declaim in public assembly, to choose a theme and expatiate on it with

telling power, and to speak convincingly and movingly in legal, religious, business, and political contexts. They enjoyed such widespread influence in the Mediterranean world, not least in Corinth, that public speakers who either could not meet their standards, or who for any reason chose not to, were viewed as seriously inferior.' Carson, *Cross,* pp. 33-34.

21. A. T. Robertson, *Word Pictures in the New Testament* (Grand Rapids: Baker Book House, 1931), vol. 4, p. 83.

22. *Ibid.,* vol. 4, p. 83.

23. C. K. Barrett, *The First Epistle to the Corinthians* (Peabody: Hendrickson Publishers, 1968), p. 65.

24. John Flavel, *The Works of John Flavel* (repr. ed., Carlisle: The Banner of Truth Trust, 1968), vol. 6, p. 572.

25. John Piper, *The Supremacy of God in Preaching* (Grand Rapids: Baker Book House, 1990), p. 33.

26. *Ibid.,* pp. 37-38.

27. J. Oswald Sanders, *Men in God's School* (London: Marshall, Morgan, and Scott, n.d.), p. 174.

28. Cited in D. Martyn Lloyd-Jones, *Studies in the Sermon on the Mount* (Grand Rapids: William B. Eerdmans Publishing Company, 1971), pp. 266-267.

29. Cited anonymously in Stott, *Portrait,* p. 124.

6

THE *SINE QUA NON* OF
GOSPEL PREACHING

The work of the Spirit, then, is joined to the word of God. But a
distinction is made, that we may know that the external word is of no
avail by itself, unless animated by the power of the Spirit ....
All power of action, then, resides in the Spirit Himself.
JOHN CALVIN

Preachers sent from God are not musical boxes which,
being once wound up, will play through their set tunes,
but they are trumpets which are utterly mute until the
living breath causes them to give forth a certain sound.
CHARLES HADDON SPURGEON

The Holy Spirit is *in* us as we preach, but he is also ever coming *to*
us. This great paradox lies at the soul of preaching. His *being in us*
and *coming to us* are the twin supports upon which God is about to
hang the cables of relationship between his world and ours.
CALVIN MILLER

The Great Awakener's First Secret
In January of 1738 the great awakener, George Whitefield, boarded
the *Whitaker,* a sailing vessel bound for America, with a view to
begin missionary work in what at the time was regarded as the
colony of Georgia. As his boat was preparing to set sail, a second
vessel, the *Samuel,* arrived in the same London harbor, having
just returned from Georgia. Of the many passengers aboard the
Samuel, one was a returning missionary: John Wesley. Providence
has provided an amazing study in contrast as the lives of those
two men crossed that day.

Whitefield, at the time, was only twenty-four years old. Even more remarkable than the tenderness of his age, however, was the breadth of impact his preaching had known throughout all of England. 'The whole nation is in an uproar,' Charles Wesley exclaimed.[1] James Hervey testified similarly: 'All London and the whole nation ring of the great things of God done by his ministry.'[2] As Whitefield boarded the *Whitaker* for Georgia he was filled with buoyancy and enthusiasm, seeing a vast spiritual harvest in his wake and eagerly anticipating even greater manifestations of the power of God.

John Wesley, on the other hand, was coming home from Georgia a broken man. His brother, Charles, having returned to London a few months prior, was equally devastated from his experiences in Georgia. Both brothers had given themselves to this missionary endeavor with the hope of earning the favor of God unto eternal life. Anticipating his ministry in Georgia, John Wesley wrote in his journal: 'My chief motive is the hope of saving my own soul.'[3] Within twenty months, however, both John and Charles had returned to London more acutely aware of their own spiritual emptiness; both suffering from ill-health and severe depression. John confessed: 'What have I learned? Why, what I the least of all suspected, that I who went to America to convert others, was never myself converted to God.'[4]

To be sure, many commonalties were shared by Whitefield and Wesley. They lived during the same period of time. They were equipped with comparable educational experiences. They both possessed significant intelligence, zeal, and discipline. Both were given to ministry in similar situations. These commonalties, however, were overshadowed by the radically different consequences that attended their efforts. Whitefield had experienced a season of significant spiritual fruitfulness. Wesley, on the contrary, despaired of life itself.

To what circumstances can these differences be attributed? The most obvious lies in the fact that Whitefield had experienced the work of regeneration, the Spirit's gift of the new birth, something that both Wesleys had yet to encounter. Even more to the point, Whitefield had experienced subsequent workings of the Spirit of God. More particularly, he had known of a blessing of the Spirit that is altogether unique to the work of preaching the gospel, a divine access of power that is given to produce divinely-intended effects in the hearers of the gospel message. His biographer asserts:

> ... Whitefield's ... effectiveness lay not in his eloquence or zeal. As we look back from our present standpoint we see that God's chosen time to 'arise and have mercy upon Zion ... yea, the set time had come,' and that in raising up Whitefield, He had granted upon him and his ministry 'a mighty effusion of the Holy Ghost'; and it was this, the Divine power, which was the first secret of his success.[5]

Whitefield had experienced what we have termed the vitality of the Holy Spirit; that is, the Spirit's effectual work of glorifying Jesus Christ through fallible men who proclaim the Christocentric scriptures. This was a fulfillment in history of the promise made by Jesus on the evening of His resurrection. His words to the disciples in Luke 24:44-48 can be summarized as follows: 'You are the witnesses of the substance set forth by the Old Testament scriptures: My death and resurrection, and the consequent forgiveness that can be found by repentant sinners. This is to be your *message*. Moreover, in the making known of this message there is a specific *method* to employ: proclaim it to all nations. Declare My redemptive accomplishments and the appropriate response to them. Finally, there is one remaining element that must not be overlooked as you give consideration to gospel ministry. Though you may cherish the central message and remain faithful to the ordained method, your mission will prove unsuccessful apart from a manifestation of the appropriate *means*.' Consequently, Jesus gives His men a pledge:

> 'And behold, I am sending forth the promise of My Father upon you; but you are to stay in the city until you are *clothed with power* from on high' (Luke 24:49).

Forty days later Jesus exhorts His disciples to this same end:

> And gathering them together, He commanded them not to leave
> Jerusalem, but to wait for what the Father had promised, 'Which,'
> He said, 'you heard of from Me; for John baptized with water, but
> you shall be baptized with the Holy Spirit not many days from now
> ... *you shall receive power* when the Holy Spirit has come upon
> you; and you shall be My witnesses both in Jerusalem, and in all
> Judea and Samaria, and even to the remotest part of the earth'
> (Acts 1:4-5, 8).

The implications of Luke 24 and Acts 1 are obvious. The
evangelical emphasis is to govern the message of the apostles
and their subsequent followers. Moreover, a particular method
is to dictate the predominant communication of this message. All
of this, however, will amount to nothing apart from the sovereign
manifestation of the necessary means. If the aim of Christian
preaching is more than intellectual enlightenment and moral
reformation, but is, instead, the thorough-going transformation of
people dead in trespasses and sins, then Christian preachers must
rest their dependence solely upon the Spirit of the living God
because such a transformation requires a power of an altogether
supernatural kind. Stated simply, the power of the Holy Spirit is
the *sine qua non* of gospel preaching, the one thing without which
nothing else matters.

It is the burden of the Apostle Paul to communicate this same
perspective in 1 Corinthians 2, a passage of which Lloyd-Jones
writes: 'I am of the opinion that for evangelicals today this chapter
is in many ways the most important single chapter in the whole
Bible'.[6] In this chapter Paul defines his apostolic ministry as one
characterized by a determination to proclaim a foolish message
and to appropriate a foolish method. Now, in verses 4-5, Paul
speaks about his *determination to rest upon a foolish means.*

The Spirit's Demonstration
In the previous chapter we gave significant consideration to the
fact that apostolic preaching involves a certain kind of style; a

style that is in identifiable harmony with the message of the cross. With regard to his preaching, Paul repeatedly reminds the Corinthians of his intentional renunciation of certain communicative techniques: 'not in cleverness of speech ... I did not come with superiority of speech or of wisdom ... not in persuasive words of wisdom' (1 Cor. 1:17; 2:1, 4). This is not to suggest that Paul refused to employ any kind of wisdom in his ministry (cf. 2:6). Nor is it to imply that Paul made no attempt to be persuasive (cf. 2 Cor. 5:11). Rather, he consciously sought to avoid any techniques that were of a manipulative nature. To be sure, Paul's aspiration is to win the hearts of people. This is his aim (to which more attention will be given in the following chapter). But in attempting to capture their affections he leaves no room for competitors. That is to say, his desire is that their hearts be captured by the gospel, not his sophisticated presentation of it. Consequently, Paul refrains from any technique of communication that, on its own merit, might elicit a response from his listeners. The implication is obvious: a response drawn out by anything other than the naked gospel simply proclaimed will, more often than not, prove to be something less than a saving response.

At this very point it is essential for preachers to give heed to Paul's methodology. To be sure, a true gospel preacher longs to see the experience of authentic conversion in the lives of the people to whom he preaches. However, he must understand that if the response of a listener is drawn out by the dimming of the lights, the playing of soft music, the powerful stories of the preacher, or the pressure of surrounding multitudes streaming forward to the altar, then it is highly unlikely that such a response will prove to be saving. Such may serve to boost the ego of the preacher, but the apostolic aim is conversion to Jesus Christ. Therefore, any technique which may confuse the latter objective with the former must be eliminated. Where the affections of people are at stake, there must be no competitors allowed. The gospel must capture their hearts, not the genius of those who seek to communicate it.

Well-meaning evangelicals may call this ministry methodology into question. 'Well,' some may say, 'I appreciate your enthusiasm. I appreciate your idealism. But I am a bird of a different feather. That is to say, both of my feet are rooted deeply in reality which means I recognize the need to be practical in order to survive. So, pastor, let me ask you, "How do you expect the gospel to succeed if you strip away all of the communicative techniques that drive every other message in our day?"' It is at this point the man of God can say with full apostolic precedence: 'I am foolish enough to expect the gospel to succeed by the means of the power of God.' About this, Paul reminds his Corinthian readers: 'And my message and my preaching were not in persuasive words of wisdom, but in demonstration of the Spirit and of power' (1 Cor. 2:4).

The word 'demonstration' means 'proof, evidence, verification'.[7] Angel asserts that through the second century this word was used in Greek culture to speak of evidence supplied by an orator to prove the validity of his argument.[8] Kistemaker refers to it as 'a term used in a court of law for testimony'.[9] It was employed in the Greek mystery religions to speak of the direct 'intervention by a divinity'.[10] Moreover, the usage of this term in extra-biblical literature reveals the efficacy of its persuasiveness. Hence, the following conclusions: 'The element of showing or demonstrating implies clearly making something known ... in a clear, convincing, and confirming manner *and therefore shown to be certain of true.*'[11] Abbott-Smith defines this term as '*certain proof.*'[12] Another suggests: '... a *compelling decision demanded* by the presupposition'.[13] Kistemaker summarizes: 'The term signifies that no one is able to refute the proof that is presented.'[14] Paul is reminding the Corinthians that his preaching was not confirmed in them as a consequence of appropriating the most current and sophisticated techniques of communication. Rather, that which caused the message to be so forcefully persuasive and convincing was the immediate intervention and power of the Holy Spirit. The phrase 'of the Spirit and of power' is a hendiadys, the coordination of two ideas, one of which is dependent upon the other.[15] The two nouns in the genitive are subjective.[16] Hence, the following captures Paul's intended meaning: the Spirit, with His power, gives the demonstration. 'My preaching,' says Paul, 'was characterized, not by manipulative techniques of communication, but by a supernatural verification that was supplied by the power of the Spirit of God.'[17]

It is this power which makes the foolish message and method effectual in the lives of people; the Holy Spirit pouring out His power on the proclamation of the Christocentric word. Luther suggests that the preacher is only a mouthpiece:

> Those who are now proclaiming the gospel are not those who really do it; they are only a mask and masquerade through which God carries out his work and will. You are not the ones who are catching fish, God says, I am drawing the net myself.[18]

Calvin indicates there is no benefit from preaching 'except when God shines in us by the light of his Spirit; and thus the inward calling, which alone is efficacious and peculiar to the elect, is distinguished from the outward voice of men'.[19] Spurgeon has referred to this work of the Spirit in preaching as 'the sacred anointing'.[20] Whitefield terms it 'the thunder and lightning'[21] in his sermons. Tony Sargent defines this 'unction' and elaborates as follows:

> ... (it is) the penetration and domination of the personality by the Spirit ... It is the preacher gliding on eagle's wings, soaring high, swooping low, carrying and being carried along by a dynamic other than his own. His consciousness of what is happening is not obliterated. He is not in a trance. He is being worked on but is aware that he is still working. He is being spoken through but he knows he is still speaking. The words are his but the facility with which they come compels him to realize that the source is beyond himself.[22]

Martyn Lloyd-Jones provides a helpful explanation:

> What is this? It is the Holy Spirit falling upon the preacher in a special manner. It is an access of power. It is God giving power, and enabling, through the Spirit, to the preacher in order that he may do

this work in a manner that lifts it beyond the efforts and endeavors of man to a position in which the preacher is being used by the Spirit and becomes the channel through whom the Spirit works.[23]

This is what we have sought to define as the vitality of the Spirit; namely, His work of glorifying Jesus Christ through fallible men who faithfully proclaim the Christocentric scriptures.

The Spirit And The Word

The scriptures repeatedly display a tight connection between the coming of the Holy Spirit and the subsequent proclamation of the word of God. This connection is seen frequently in the Old Testament scriptures. In Numbers 11, as a fulfillment of God's promise to Moses, the Holy Spirit is given to the seventy elders of Israel, with the attendant manifestation of their prophesying. Jealous for the unique position of Moses, Joshua emphatically pleads with his mentor to restrain the seventy elders. The response of Moses is telling: 'Are you jealous for my sake? Would that all the LORD's people were prophets, that the LORD would put His Spirit upon them!' (Num. 11:29). The implied connection between the gift of the Holy Spirit and the subsequent communication of the prophetic word is evident. Numbers 24 records the coming of the Spirit upon Balaam with the result that the word of the Lord is made known through him (Num. 24:2ff). In his final song, King David declares: 'The Spirit of the LORD spoke by me, and His word was on my tongue' (2 Sam. 23:2). In 2 Chronicles this relationship of the Spirit to the proclaimed word is cited again: 'Then the Spirit of God came on Zechariah the son of Jehoiada the priest; and he stood above the people and said to them, "Thus God has said ..." ' (2 Chr. 24:20). Nehemiah 9 sets forth the penitent prayer of the people of Israel which recounts their repeated failures and Yahweh's subsequent mercy: '... Thou didst bear with them for many years, and admonished them by Thy Spirit through Thy prophets' (Neh. 9:30). The prophet Ezekiel writes: 'Then the Spirit of the LORD fell upon me, and He said, "Say, 'Thus says the LORD ...' " ' (Ezek. 11:5). Several other references could be cited which reveal the relationship between the coming of the Holy Spirit and the consequent proclamation of the word of God. It can be argued that a predominant ministry of the Holy Spirit as recorded in the Old Testament scriptures is His coming upon men for the purpose of making known the word of God.[24]

The New Testament scriptures continue to reveal a connection between the coming of the Spirit of God and the proclamation of the word of God. A specific phrase in Luke-Acts appears eight times and always in relationship to a prophetic kind of speaking. The verb used in each of these occurrences is πίμπλημι ('that which fills or takes possession of the mind').[25] In each of these occurrences πίμπλημι appears in an aoristic tense and with a passive voice. Hence, each usage of the phrase can be rendered: 'filled with the Holy Spirit', or 'having been filled with the Holy Spirit'. In each of these eight occurrences the filling of the Spirit is presented as an *event,* a sovereign and spontaneous act of God related to the proclamation of truth.[26] At this point it is necessary to give brief consideration to each of these passages. The first appears in relationship to the birth announcement of John the Baptist:

> But the angel said to him, 'Do not be afraid, Zacharias, for your petition has been heard, and your wife Elizabeth will bear you a son, and you will give him the name John. And you will have joy and gladness, and many will rejoice at his birth. For he will be great in the sight of the Lord, and he will drink no wine or liquor; and he will *be filled with the Holy Spirit,* while yet in his mother's womb' (Luke 1:13-15).

Gabriel continues by indicating that this 'filling' is directly connected to the specific ministry given to John: 'And he will turn back many of the sons of Israel to the Lord their God. And it is he who will go as a forerunner before Him in the spirit and power of Elijah ...' (Luke 1:16-17). John's prophetic ministry of repentance, like unto that of Elijah, necessitated the filling of the Spirit of God. Here is a direct parallel to what was repeatedly seen in the Old Testament: the coming upon of the Holy Spirit for the purpose of proclaiming God's word.

The second and third appearances of this phrase concern Elizabeth and Zacharias, the parents of John the Baptist:

> Now at this time Mary arose and went with haste to the hill country, to a city of Judah, and entered the house of Zacharias and greeted Elizabeth. And it came about that when Elizabeth heard Mary's greeting, the baby leaped in her womb; and Elizabeth *was filled with the Holy Spirit* (Luke 1:39-41).

What follows this sudden 'filling of the Spirit?' Elizabeth prophetically proclaims Mary to be the mother of the promised Messiah:

> And she cried out with a loud voice, and said, 'Blessed among women are you, and blessed is the fruit of your womb! And how has it happened to me, that the mother of my Lord should come to me ...' (Luke 1:42-45).

When the Baptist is born, his father, Zacharias, has a similar experience:

> And his father Zacharias *was filled with the Holy Spirit,* and prophesied, saying: 'Blessed be the Lord God of Israel, For He has visited us and accomplished redemption for His people ...' (Luke 1:67-79).

Here, again, a sudden filling of the Holy Spirit results in the proclamation of a word that has a supernatural origin.

The fourth usage of this phrase appears in the earliest portion of the book of Acts. Prior to His ascension Jesus reinforces the promise previously made to His disciples: '... you shall receive power when the Holy Spirit has come upon you; and you shall be My witnesses ...' (Acts 1:8). On the Day of Pentecost this promise comes to fulfillment:

And suddenly there came from heaven a noise like a violent, rushing wind, and it filled the whole house where they were sitting. And there appeared to them tongues as of fire distributing themselves, and they rested on each one of them. And they *were all filled with the Holy Spirit* and began to speak with other tongues, as the Spirit was giving them utterance (Acts 2:2-4).

Issuing forth as a consequence of the filling of the Spirit is a supernatural kind of speaking. Luke, however, does not have unintelligible 'languages' in view. Rather, these 'tongues' were quite understandable and their content specifically focused:

And when this sound occurred, the multitude came together, and were bewildered, because they were each one hearing them speak in his own language .... 'And how is it that we each hear them in our own language to which we were born ... we hear them in our own tongues speaking of the mighty deeds of God' (Acts 2:6, 8, 11).

The Pentecostal manifestation of 'tongues' amounts to the proclamation of the redemptive accomplishments of the triune God in languages understood by the assembled hearers. Peter then proceeds to legitimize this experience by quoting an Old Testament revelation:

'but this is what was spoken of through the prophet Joel: "And it shall be in the last days," God says, "that I will pour forth of My Spirit upon all mankind; and your sons and your daughters shall prophesy ..."' (Acts 2:16-17).

One of the effects of the new covenant advent of the Spirit would be the making known of the word of God in a greater and more profusive fashion.

This phrase is employed by Luke on a fifth occasion in Acts 4 in relationship to the imprisonment of Peter and John. Following the healing of a man lame from birth (Acts 3:1-8), Peter and John begin to proclaim Jesus and His resurrection from the dead. This preaching leads to their arrest. On the following day they are placed before the Jewish leadership and asked to supply an explanation for this healing: 'By what power, or in what name, have you done this?' (Acts 4:7). Luke then records: 'Then Peter, *filled with the Holy Spirit,* said to them ...' (Acts 4:8). But the attentive reader will ask the obvious question: 'Was not Peter filled with the Holy Spirit in Acts 2:4? What, then, is this?' While it must be affirmed that all Christians are indwelt by the Holy Spirit permanently (cf. John 14:16; Rom. 8:9), and all believers will experience the effects of the Spirit's presence in their lives to a greater or lesser degree (particularly as it relates to the transformation of the character into Christlikeness, cf. Gal. 5:16-24), there is another work of the Spirit directly related to the proclamation of the word of God, a unique filling of the Holy Spirit which amounts to an access of His power. This is a spontaneous work of God attending the declaration of His word which is given sovereignly and selectively.

Later in chapter 4 Luke employs this phrase on a sixth occasion. When Peter and John are released by the Jewish leadership they return to their fellow disciples. Luke then records the following experience:

> And when they had prayed, the place where they had gathered together was shaken, and they *were all filled with the Holy Spirit,* and began to speak the word of God with boldness (Acts 4:31).

As in the aforementioned scenario with Peter, these believers were Christians in the full New Testament sense. That is to say, they had been recipients of the indwelling Spirit of God. And yet, they are suddenly 'filled with the Holy Spirit', with the result that the word of God is spoken with great boldness.

The seventh usage of this phrase relates to the experience of the Apostle Paul in Acts 9. Here, Ananias informs the recently converted Saul that he has been sent by the command of the Lord Jesus so that Saul might regain his sight and 'be filled with the Holy Spirit' (Acts 9:17). The reason for Paul's need of filling is implied from verse 15, where the Lord tells Ananias that Saul 'is a chosen instrument of Mine, to bear My name before the

Gentiles and kings and the sons of Israel' (Acts 9:15). Furthermore, this is confirmed by Paul's later recollection of Ananias' words:

> And he said, 'The God of our fathers has appointed you to know His will, and to see the Righteous One, and to hear an utterance from His mouth. For you will be a witness for Him to all men of what you have seen and heard' (Acts 22:14-15).

It is no surprise, then, that after Paul received this filling of the Spirit Luke records the following: 'and immediately he began to proclaim Jesus in the synagogues, saying, "He is the Son of God"' (Acts 9:20).

Finally, Luke draws upon this phrase on an eighth occasion. In Acts 13 Paul and Barnabas are preaching the gospel on the island of Salamis. While there, a Roman proconsul named Sergius Paulus summons them that he might hear the word of God:

> But Elymas the magician (for thus his name is translated) was opposing them, seeking to turn the proconsul away from the faith. But Saul, who was also known as Paul, *filled with the Holy Spirit*, fixed his gaze upon him, and said ... (Acts 13:8-11).

Here is Paul, a Christian and an apostle. He is a man possessing the indwelling Holy Spirit. Moreover, he is man who on at least one previous occasion had been filled with the Spirit of God. Right here, however, Luke records another occasion of this filling. Consequently, once again Paul speaks under the Spirit's direct influence.

What is this 'Spirit-filling'? An examination of these eight passages reveal it to be an instantaneous, sudden, and sovereign operation of the Spirit of God coming upon a man so that his proclamation of Jesus Christ might be attended by holy power. This, then, appears to be the emphasis of Paul's words when he says to the Corinthians: 'And my message and my preaching were not in persuasive words of wisdom, *but in demonstration of the Spirit and of power*' (1 Cor. 2:4). The Spirit, by the means of

His power, through the words of a preacher, establishes, veri-
fies, and confirms the gospel in the heart of a man so that he must
respond to the truth he hears. Paul conveys the same idea elsewhere:

> And we proclaim Him, admonishing every man and teaching every
> man with all wisdom, that we may present every man complete in
> Christ. And for this purpose also I labor, striving *according to His
> power, which mightily works within me* (Col. 1:28-29).

> for our gospel did not come to you in word only, *but also in power
> and in the Holy Spirit* and with full conviction (1 Thess. 1:5).

Peter similarly adds:

> It was revealed to them that they were not serving themselves, but
> you, in these things which now have been announced to you through
> those who preached the gospel to you *by the Holy Spirit sent from
> heaven* ... (1 Pet. 1:12).

Martyn Lloyd-Jones refers to this work of the Spirit as 'the smile
of God'[27] upon the preacher. To be sure, there are occasions
when the preacher himself is conscious of this attending power
in the act of preaching. More often than not, however, it is the
congregation that recognizes the voice of the Spirit of God.

> Ministers may give voice and utterance to the Bible which is the
> word of God. Like James and John they may be sons of thunder to
> impenitent sinners. They may pour forth a tempest of impassioned,
> eloquent declamation. They may proclaim all the terrors of the Lord;
> represent the earth as quaking and trembling under the footsteps of
> Jehovah; flash around them the lightnings of Sinai; borrow, as it
> were, the trump of the archangel, and summon the living and the
> dead to the bar of God ... and still God may not be there; his voice
> may not be heard either in the tempest, the earthquake, or the fire;
> and if so, the preacher will have labored but in vain; his hearers,
> though they may for the moment be affected, will receive no per-
> manent salutary impressions. Nothing effectual can be done unless

God be there, unless he speaks with his still, small voice. By this
still, small voice we mean the voice of God's Spirit; the voice
which speaks not only to man, but in man; the voice, which, in
stillness and silence, whispers to the ear of the soul, and presses
upon the conscience those great eternal truths, a knowledge and
belief which is connected with salvation .... Large congregations
often sit and hear a message from God, while perhaps not a single
individual among them feels that the message is addressed to himself, or that he has any personal concern in it. But it is not so when
God speaks with his still, small voice. Every one, to whom God
thus speaks, whether he be alone, or in the midst of a large assembly, feels that he is spoken to, that he is called, as it were, by name.
The message comes home to him, and says as Nathan said to David,
Thou art the man. Hence, while multitudes are around him, he sits
as if he were alone. At him alone the preacher seems to aim. On
him alone his eye seems to be fixed. To him alone every word
seems to come .... No scene, on this side of the bar of God, can be
more awfully, overpoweringly solemn, than the scene which such
an assembly exhibits. The Father of spirits is present to the spirits
he has made; present to each of them, and speaking to each. Each
one feels that the eye of God is upon him, that the voice of God is
speaking to him. Each one therefore, though surrounded by numbers, mourns solitary and apart. The powers of the world to come
are felt. Eternity, with all its crushing realities, opens to view, and
descends upon the mind. The final sentence, though uttered by
human lips, comes with scarcely less weight, than if pronounced by
the Judge himself. All countenances gather blackness, and a stillness, solemn and profound, and awful, pervades the place, inter-
rupted only by a stifled sob, or a half repressed sigh. My hearers,
such scenes have been witnessed. Within a very few years they
have been witnessed in hundreds of places.[28]

It may be surprising for some to discover that when the Spirit
of God powerfully attends the preaching of the word, one of the
common indicators is a heightened sense of quiet; not shouts and
ecstasies, but rather an unnatural silence. The ever-present cough-
ing ceases. The incessant movement of people is overcome by a
dramatic stillness. And suddenly, though the features of the
preacher's face and the timbre of his voice are still identifiably

his, the words coming forth from his mouth seem to have been sent from heaven itself.

Near the conclusion of his excellent book on preaching John Stott provides an illustration worthy of great consideration:

> I have before me, as I write, a photograph of the massive central pulpit from which Spurgeon preached in the Metropolitan Tabernacle. The photograph is reproduced in the second volume of his *Autobiography*. Fifteen steps led up to it on each side, in a great sweeping curve, and I have heard it said (but have been unable to confirm) that as Spurgeon mounted those stairs, with the measured tread of a heavily built man, he muttered to himself on each one, 'I believe in the Holy Ghost.' We may be quite sure that, after fifteen repetitions of this creedal affirmation, by the time he entered the pulpit, he *did* believe in the Holy Spirit. He also urges us to do the same ...[29]

As one preacher to another, allow me to ask you directly: Is this what you affirm when you wake up on the Lord's Day morning? *'I believe in the Holy Ghost.'* Is this what you affirm when you drive into the church parking lot? *'I believe in the Holy Ghost.'* Is this what you affirm when you kneel in your study just before entering into the sanctuary? *'I believe in the Holy Ghost.'* Is this what you affirm when, with all of your overwhelming limitations, you step behind the sacred desk to proclaim the majestic infinities of Jesus Christ? *'I believe in the Holy Ghost.'* Do you long for the voice of God to be heard when you preach? Then this must be your credo: *'I believe in the Holy Ghost.'*

It is not enough to possess the proper message. Nor is it enough to embrace the proper method. Gospel preachers desperately need the divinely appointed means; the clothing with power from on high.

O God, on the basis of the merits of Your Son, give us this.

Notes

1. Luke Tyerman, *The Life and Times of the Rev. John Wesley, M. A.* (London: Hodder and Stoughton, 1870), vol. 1, p. 112.

2. _____, *The Oxford Methodists: Memoirs of Clayton, Ingham, Gambold, Hervey and Broughton* (London: Hodder and Stoughton, 1873), p. 215.

3. John Wesley, *The Journal of John Wesley* (London: The Epworth Press, 1938), vol. 8, p. 288.

4. *Ibid.*, vol. 1, p. 422.

5. Arnold Dallimore, *George Whitefield: The Life and Times of the Great Evangelist of the 18th Century Revival* (Carlisle: The Banner of Truth Trust, 1980), vol. 1, pp. 116-117.

6. D. M. Lloyd-Jones, *Authority* (repr. ed., Carlisle: The Banner of Truth Trust, 1992), p. 85.

7. Johannes P. Louw and Eugene A. Nida, *Greek-English Lexicon of the New Testament Based on Semantic Domains* (New York: United Bible Societies, 1989), vol. 1, p. 341.

8. G. T. D. Angel, '$\dot{\alpha}\pi o\delta\epsilon\iota\xi\iota s$,' *The New International Dictionary of New Testament Theology,* ed. Colin Brown (Grand Rapids: Zondervan Publishing House, 1979), vol. 3, p. 570.

9. Simon J. Kistemaker, *Exposition of the First Epistle to the Corinthians* (Grand Rapids: Baker Book House, 1993), p. 76.

10. William F. Arndt and F. Wilbur Gingrich, *A Greek-English Lexicon of the New Testament and Other Early Christian Literature* (Chicago: The University of Chicago Press, 1979), p. 89.

11. Louw and Nida, *Semantic Domains,* vol. 1, p. 341.

12. G. Abbott Smith, *A Manual Greek Lexicon of the New Testament* (Edinburgh: T & T Clark, 1981), p. 49.

13. Fritz Rienecker, *A Linguistic Key to the Greek New Testament* (Grand Rapids: Zondervan Publishing House, 1980), p. 390.

14. Kistemaker, *Corinthians,* p. 76.

15. See F. Blass and A. Debrunner, *A Greek Grammar of the New Testament and Other Early Christian Literature* (Chicago: The University of Chicago Press, 1961), p. 228.

16. The nouns in the genitive ($\pi\nu\epsilon\dot{\nu}\mu\alpha\tau os$ $\kappa\alpha\iota$ $\delta\nu\nu\dot{\alpha}\mu\epsilon\omega s$) act as the subject of, or do the action implied in the noun to which they stand related ($\dot{\alpha}\pi o\delta\epsilon\acute{\iota}\xi\epsilon\iota$).

17. Here we discover the trinitarian basis for a New Testament preaching ministry: gospel preachers proclaim *God's* testimony, concerning His *Son,* verified by the power of the *Holy Spirit.*

18. Martin Luther, *Luther's Works* (St. Louis: Concordia Press, 1956), vol. 17, pp. 262-263.

19. John Calvin, *Commentaries on the Epistle of Paul the Apostle to*

the Romans (Edinburgh: Calvin Translation Society, 1849), pp. 400-401.

20. Charles Haddon Spurgeon, *Lectures to my Students* (repr. ed., Pasadena: Pilgrim Publications, 1990), p. 96.

21. Cited without reference by D. M. Lloyd-Jones, *The Puritans: Their Origins and Successors* (Carlisle: The Banner of Truth Trust, 1987), p.122.

22. Tony Sargent, *The Sacred Anointing* (Wheaton: Crossway Books, 1994), p. 29.

23. D. Martyn Lloyd-Jones, *Preaching and Preachers* (Grand Rapids: Zondervan Publishing House, 1971), p. 305.

24. 'Here (the Old Testament) ... He (the Spirit of God) is presented as the source of all the supernatural powers and activities which are directed to the foundation and preservation and development of the kingdom of God in the midst of the wicked world ....We are moving here in a distinctly supernatural atmosphere and the activities which come under review belong to an entirely supernatural order ....Prominent above all other theocratic gifts of the Spirit, however, are the gifts of supernatural knowledge and insight, culminating in the great gift of Prophecy. This greatest of gifts ... is the free gift of the Spirit of God to special organs chosen for the purpose of the revelation of His will', Benjamin Breckinridge Warfield, *Biblical Doctrines* (repr. ed., Grand Rapids: Baker Book House, 1991), pp. 112, 114. See also Wilf Hildebrandt, *An Old Testament Theology of the Spirit of God* (Peabody: Hendrickson Publishers, 1995), pp. 151-192.

25. Abbott-Smith, *A Manual Greek Lexicon,* p. 360.

26. This must not be confused with a similar phrase that appears six times in Luke-Acts (Luke 4:1; Acts 6:3, 5; 7:55; 11:24; 13:52). In each of these occurrences either the adjective $\pi\lambda\eta\rho\eta\varsigma$ ('full') or the verb $\pi\lambda\eta\rho\acute{o}\omega$ ('to make full', or 'to fill') is used. See Arndt and Gingrich, *A Greek-English Lexicon,* pp. 669-670. These phrases, in contradistinction with the aforementioned eight phrases, refer to *an abiding state or condition of fulness over against an event of being filled.* Using Acts 4:8 as an example Bruce states: 'We should distinguish between this use of the aorist passive, denoting a special moment of inspiration, and the use of the adjective *pleres* ('full') to denote the abiding character of the Spirit-filled man (cf. Stephen in 6:5). F. F. Bruce, *Commentary on the Book of Acts* (Grand Rapids: William B. Eerdmans Publishing Company, 1970), p. 99.

A distinction should also be made between these eight phrases and the singular Pauline phrase in Ephesians 5:18, 'be filled with the Spirit', which employs the present passive imperative of $\pi\lambda\eta\rho\acute{o}\omega$. Moreover, in all the Luke-Acts passages the genitive is used ($\pi\nu\epsilon\acute{u}\mu\alpha\tau o\varsigma\ \acute{a}\gamma\acute{i}ov$), the case typically employed with verbs of filling to stress the *content* of whatever is being filled. See Blass and A. Debrunner, *A Greek Grammar,* p. 95. In contrast, the Pauline text employs the dative ($\pi\nu\epsilon\acute{u}\mu\alpha\tau\iota$) with the preposition $\acute{\epsilon}\nu$, supplying a locative emphasis. Hence, the verse could be translated 'be filled in (the) Spirit', *i.e.,* 'be filled in the realm of the Spirit/ spirit', which, as the context makes clear, will consequently issue forth in certain behaviors (5:19-21). A second possibility for this phrase exists if $\acute{\varepsilon}v$ with the dative is taken in an instrumental sense: 'be filled with (by means of) the Spirit'. In other words, the Holy Spirit is not the content of the filling, but the instrument God uses to fill the believer with some other content. In summary, the New Testament never employs $\acute{\varepsilon}v\ \pi\nu\varepsilon\acute{v}\mu\alpha\tau\iota$ to express the content with which something is filled.

27. D. Martyn Lloyd-Jones, *Revival* (Wheaton: Crossway Books, 1987), p. 295.

28. Edward Payson, 'God Heard in the Still Small Voice', as cited in Iain Murray, *Revival and Revivalism: The Making and Marring of American Evangelicalism* (Carlisle: The Banner of Truth Trust, 1994), pp. 212-213.

29. John R. W. Stott, *Between Two Worlds: The Art of Preaching in the Twentieth Century* (Grand Rapids: William B. Eerdmans Publishing Company, 1982), p. 334.

7

THE OCCUPATIONAL
VULNERABILITY OF PREACHING

We preach and pray, and you hear; but there is no motion Christ-
ward until the Spirit of God blows upon them.
JOHN FLAVEL

Always aim at effect.
CHARLES HADDON SPURGEON

Many who for the first time come under the sound of
Holy Ghost preaching are mortally offended because while
they may consider themselves expert sermon-tasters, having
much experience of eloquent preaching, they have never
been exposed to the white light of the Spirit.
WILLIAM STILL

The Preacher's Inescapable Frustration

The preacher, while, like other speakers, he has the power to inform and excite an audience, has not power in himself to compass
the great aim of preaching. The aim of preaching is different from
that of other public speaking. It looks deeper. It would renew and
cleanse the heart. If it fails there, it fails entirely. And fail it will
without the accompanying 'power from on high'. The renewal of
the soul is what no man, with all wealth of learning and scholarship,
and of cultivated taste and oratorical power, can accomplish. It is
'not by might, nor by power, but by my Spirit,' saith the Lord. A
sermon may be constructed after the best models; it may conform
to all the rules of homiletics; the text may be suitable and fruitful;

the plan may be faultless; the execution may discover genius and judgment; there may be accurate analysis and strong reasoning; proof and motive; solidity and beauty; logic and passion; argument direct and indirect; perspicuity, purity, correctness, propriety, precision; description, antithesis, metaphor, allegory, comparison; motives from goodness, motives from happiness, motives from self-love; appeals to the sense of the beautiful, the sense of right, to the affections, the passions, the emotions; a sermon may be all this, and yet that very sermon, even though it fell from the lips of a prince of pulpit oratory, were as powerless in the renewal of a soul as in raising of the dead, if unaccompanied by the omnipotent energy of the Holy Ghost.[1]

From the very first reading of this quotation I found its earliest sentences to be exceedingly ominous in that they capture the occupational vulnerability of the gospel preacher:

'The preacher, while, like other speakers, he has the power to inform and excite an audience, *has not power in himself to compass the great aim of preaching.* The aim of preaching is different from that of other public speaking. It looks deeper. It would renew and cleanse the heart. *If it fails there, it fails entirely.*'

The true gospel preacher lives with a nagging frustration; a vulnerability that haunts him daily. To be sure, there are moments when other concerns occupy his attention. Sooner or later, however, his mind inevitably returns to an annoying recognition: he is possessed by a desire to accomplish an objective that he will never be able to accomplish if left to himself. At times, the awareness of this dilemma is overwhelming. He is thoroughly acquainted with the cry of Isaiah the prophet: 'Who has believed our message?' (Isa. 53:1). Certain Sundays leave him with a forced conclusion to this question left intentionally unanswered: 'It seems that no one has.' The cause of his anguish is not just that his ego has been bruised (though, most assuredly, this accounts for some of it!); rather, the recognition that he has fallen short of the aim placed within his heart by God Himself. For this reason, many Christian preachers have sought to redefine the aim of Christian preaching.

What is the aim of Christian preaching, the objective to which all evangelical proclamation is directed? The aim of Christian preaching is the glory and honor of Jesus Christ through the means of the saving and sanctifying of sinners. This is the evangelical objective. The dilemma for the preacher, however, is that this objective can never be achieved apart from a source of power external to himself. Herein, then, is the cause of the preacher's occupational vulnerability: he is a man possessed by a holy compulsion but hobbled by human inability.

In the previous chapter, the relationship of the Spirit to the proclamation of God's truth was established. Specific attention was given to the Old Testament scriptures which set forth repeated accounts of the Spirit's coming upon a man for the purpose of declaring the word of God through him. Moreover, it was discovered that the New Testament supplies a record of the experience of believers who were 'filled with the Holy Spirit', consequently resulting in the communication of truth established and verified by the Spirit's power. There can be no question that throughout all of the scriptures there appears an intimate connection between the coming of the Spirit and the subsequent proclamation of the word.

The most significant illustration of this connection, however, can be observed from the earliest days of the public ministry of Jesus Christ. At the inception of His ministry Jesus is baptized by his cousin, John. Luke records the occasion as follows: 'and while He was praying, heaven was opened, and *the Holy Spirit descended upon Him* in bodily form like a dove ...' (Luke 3:21-22). Luke then describes Jesus as 'full of the Holy Spirit' and that He 'was led about by the Spirit' (Luke 4:1). Following His temptation Luke indicates that Jesus returned to Galilee 'in the power of the Spirit' (Luke 4:14). Then, four verses later, Jesus speaks these words in the synagogue at Nazareth:

> '*The Spirit of the Lord is upon Me,* because He anointed Me to *preach* the gospel to the poor. He has sent Me to *proclaim* release to the captives, and recovery of sight to the blind, to set free those

who are downtrodden, to *proclaim* the favorable year of the Lord'
(Luke 4:18-19).

Certainly, at this very point, great mystery is apparent. The nature
of the hypostatic union is unquestionably one of the most complex
theological doctrines in all of sacred scripture, rivaled only by
the revelation of God's three-in-oneness. Evangelicals readily
affirm the Son of God as co-equal and co-eternal with God the
Father: 'God of God, Light of Light, very God of very God.' Yet,
as the Son of Man in His mediatorial role, this anointing of the
Spirit of God was necessary *in direct relationship to His work
of preaching.* Whether or not this easily meets with our highly
rationalized views of the incarnation is irrelevant. The Messiah,
by His own admission, was given the Spirit of God (cf. John
3:34, 'without measure') for the purpose of carrying out His
ministry of proclaiming the gospel.

The conclusion must be obvious. If, for the effectual heralding
of the word of God, such an endowment of power proved
necessary for the prophets of the Old Testament, the apostles and
other Christians of the New Testament, and even the incarnate
Son of God Himself, how much more will such power be
necessary for contemporary preachers of the gospel?

In the Christian system unction is the anointing of the Holy Ghost
... the one divine enablement by which the preacher accomplishes
the peculiar and saving ends of preaching .... This divine unction on
the preacher generates through the word of God the spiritual results
that flow from the gospel ... it is the one distinguishing feature that
separates true gospel preaching from all other methods of present-
ing truth. It backs and interpenetrates the revealed truth with all the
force of God .... Without this unction on the preacher the gospel
has no more power to propagate itself than any other system of
truth. This is the seal of its divinity. Unction in the preacher puts
God in the gospel .... It is in this element that the pulpit oftener fails
than in any other element. Just at this all-important point it lapses.
Learning it may have, brilliancy and eloquence may delight and
charm, sensation or less offensive methods may bring the populace

in crowds, mental power may impress and enforce truth with all its resources; but without this unction, each and all these will be but as a fretful assault of the waters on a Gibraltar. Spray and foam may cover and spangle; but the rocks are there still, unimpressed and unimpressible. The human heart can no more be swept of its hardness and sin by these human forces than these rocks can be swept away by the ocean's ceaseless flow.[2]

The Aim Which Justifies The Means

Why should Christian preachers intentionally renounce all forms of human communication that can be subsumed under the headings of 'cleverness of speech, superiority of speech, wisdom, persuasive words of wisdom' (1 Cor. 1:17; 2:1, 4)? Why should these 'trans-generational' approaches be set aside in lieu of the 'demonstration of the Spirit and of power' (1 Cor. 2:4), especially when one considers the responses they often arouse? Stated simply, *the aim of Christian preaching determines the means we employ.* Paul informs the Corinthians that the nature of his objective established the indispensability of the appointed means:

> And my message and my preaching were not in persuasive words of wisdom, but in demonstration of the Spirit and of power, that your faith should not rest on the **wisdom** of men, but on the power of God (1 Cor. 2:4-5).

It is possible for faith to be generated by a source other than that which is divine. When this occurs, however, such faith will not display saving integrity. Rather, it is the product of what Paul defines as 'the wisdom of men'. Eventually it will manifest the weakness of its source, in much the same way a lifeless plant can reveal the poor quality of the soil in which it exists. If faith is drawn out by the air-tight logic of a preacher, the emotionally-charged manipulations of a singer, or the marketing techniques of the seeker-sensitive movement, then it will prove vulnerable to someone possessing a more intelligent argument, a more moving presentation, or a persuasive approach that is more exceedingly self-centered. Certainly, for example, there are advocates of Islam that are more intelligent, articulate, and zealous than many Christians. Surely there are proponents of the theory of evolution who are much more persuasive than Christians who espouse creation as a divine fiat. If the advancement of Christianity depends upon the intellectual prowess of its adherents, then the kingdom of God is doomed to certain failure. Moreover, of all people, God Himself would be most foolish. Why is this so? Because of the gross limitations inherent in the people He chooses as His own (cf. 1 Cor. 1:26-28). For this very reason careful consideration, and even caution, needs to be given to evangelistic approaches that are built upon apologetic emphases. For example, it is common for Christian student groups on college campuses to sponsor debates between Christians and non-Christians with the well-meaning intention of winning adherents to Christianity. Often advertisements take the following form:

Join us at 2:00pm in the Student Union
on Friday afternoon
as we debate the historicity of the
resurrection of Jesus Christ.

Such a scenario, however, creates the possibility of at least two outcomes, neither of which is favorable to the cause of the gospel. One outcome may be the resounding defeat of the Christian advocate by a clear-headed unbeliever. Such a possibility can in no way be attractive to any true Christian. The second outcome may see the overwhelming victory of the Christian, which, as a result, may draw out superficial interest on the part of some unbelievers in the audience. 'Well,' it might be asked, 'what could be so terribly wrong with such an outcome?' But what will be the consequence of the 'faith' of such a person when the Christian who first aroused his interest is eventually defeated by an unbeliever of superior intelligence? Most likely, it will readily give way to the more intelligent presentation because its allegiance was predicated upon the presupposition that Christianity is more intellectually superior than all other religious philosophies or ideals. 'What depends upon a clever argument is at the mercy of a cleverer argument.'[3] Bloesch rightly exhorts:

> As messengers and ambassadors of our Lord Jesus Christ we do not so much persuade people of the truth of the gospel as invite them to believe in the gospel. We should not expend our efforts on arguments in support of the faith (though these are not to be disregarded altogether) but proclaim a message that creates the possibility of faith. We can persuade insiders of the viability of our theological interpretations, but we cannot persuade outsiders of the credibility of the gospel. Our task is not to *argue* the case for the gospel, as though it needed our defense, but to *present* the gospel as the life-giving message that can alone redeem from sin and death .... We must be prepared to give answers to those who question the claims of faith (1 Pet. 3:15-16), but we should bear in mind that no human explanation can move the hearts of hardened sinners, though indeed they may be prompted to inquire further and perhaps finally hear and grasp the mystery of God's unfathomable love as revealed in Jesus Christ. *Yet this inward hearing and grasping are themselves gifts of the Holy Spirit, who works through the preached word of the cross* (Rom. 10:14-17). God gives not only faith but the very condition to receive it.[4]

Elsewhere Bloesch states:

> Biblical preaching ... will not seek to defend the validity of the claims of the Christian religion but instead herald the good news of reconciliation and redemption through the death and resurrection of Jesus Christ. Our task is simply to let down the net (the gospel), and Christ will bring in the fish (Luke 5:1-10) .... We do not need to prove scripture but to expound scripture in the light of its goal and content—the cross of Christ. We are not called to discover a point of contact with our hearers, since the word of God creates its own response. God sends forth his word, and it does not return to him void (Isa. 55:11). Neither should we seek to correlate the gospel message with the questions of our hearers (as Tillich and Brunner advise); rather we should so confront them with the gospel that they are moved to ask the right questions. We are to begin with the word of God in scripture and then relate it to the cultural situation;

we do not begin with man's existential predicament and then try to discover whether scripture throws any light upon it.[5]

The burden of Paul is to make clear that Christian faith is not the result of a man's brilliance or skills of argumentation. Rather, it is a consequence of the power of God attending the proclamation of Jesus Christ and Him crucified.[6] 'When I arrived in Corinth,' Paul recollects, 'I was bound to a foolish message, method, and means. Why was this the case? Because of the target at which I was aiming. I wanted your faith to be generated, not by man's wisdom, but by God's power.' Such a faith, in contrast to that which is the product of human ingenuity, will always prove invincible. Hence, Hodge states:

> The design of the apostle in acting as stated in the preceding verse, was that the faith of his hearers might not rest on human reason, but on the testimony of God. It might have been easy for him to argue the Corinthians into a conviction of the truth of the gospel, by appealing to its superiority to heathenism and to the evidence of its divine origin afforded by prophecy and miracles. He might have exhibited the folly of idolatry, and the absurdity of pagan rites and ceremonies, and convinced them of the historical truth of Christianity. The conviction thus produced would be rational and important; but it would not be saving faith. Faith founded on such evidence is merely speculative. The true foundation of faith, or rather, the foundation of true faith, is *the power of God*. This is explained by what he had before called 'the demonstration of the Spirit'. That exercise of divine power, therefore, to which he refers as the ground of faith, is the powerful operation of the Spirit, bearing witness with and by the truth in our hearts. A faith which is founded on the authority of the church, or upon arguments addressed to the understanding, or even on the moral power of the truth as it affects the natural conscience ... is unstable and inoperative. But a faith founded on the demonstration of the Spirit is abiding, infallible, and works by love and purifies the heart.[7]

The aim of gospel preaching must never be a superficial response drawn out by crafty arguments and manipulative persuasiveness. Such an aim is too low. Moreover, it is not a salvific aim. Our aim, on the other hand, is that the faith of sinners be a real and saving faith, resting entirely upon the person and work of Jesus Christ. This kind of faith, however, originates only as the consequence of what Paul terms a 'demonstration', a kind of internal evidence granted by the power of the Spirit of God. When a sinner renounces his rebellion against the Lord of Glory and willingly embraces Him by faith, it is not a consequence of the exceptional abilities of the preacher. Rather, conversion has occurred because it pleased the sovereign Holy Spirit to exercise His saving power in liaison with the proclamation of the Christocentric scriptures. The aim of Christian preaching justifies the means we seek.

Effects And The Sovereign Spirit
What effects can we expect to see when the proclamation of the gospel is attended by the power of the Spirit? In part, sinners, previously unable to respond in any positive fashion, now readily embrace Jesus Christ for forgiveness of sins and the gift of eternal life. From the perspective of God's eternal purpose the same experience may be expressed in different terms:

> We give thanks to God always for all of you, making mention of you in our prayers; constantly bearing in mind your work of faith and labor of love and steadfastness of hope in our Lord Jesus Christ in the presence of our God and Father, knowing, brethren beloved by God, *His choice of you; for our gospel did not come to you in word only, but also in power and in the Holy Spirit and with full conviction* ... (1 Thess. 1:2-5).

The elect are distinguished as those to whom the gospel comes in power. Repentance and faith are the consequent responses:

> ... having received the word in much tribulation with the joy of the Holy Spirit ... you turned to God from idols to serve a living and true God ... when you received from us the word of God's message, you accepted it not as the word of men, but for what it really

is, the word of God, which also performs its work in you who believe (1 Thess. 1:6, 9; 2:13).

Is this to suggest that conversions will always be forthcoming
whenever the Spirit empowers a preacher of the gospel? No, it is
not. Firstly, the vitality of the Spirit is not exclusive to evangelistic
settings. His accompanying power may, and often does, attend
preaching where only believers are present (cf. Acts 4:30).
Secondly, there are occasions in the book of Acts where no
mention of conversions is recorded following evangelistic
preaching that has been attended by the power of the Spirit (cf.
Acts 4:13ff.).

There is, however, a discernible experience that appears to
accompany Spirit-empowered preaching. Following Peter's
sermon before the Sanhedrin in Acts 4, the sentiment of the Council
is recorded: 'Now as they observed the *confidence* of Peter'
(Acts 4:13). Later in the chapter, when the believers are gathered
for prayer they petition God for this same gift: 'And now, Lord
... grant that Thy bond-servants may speak Thy word with all
confidence' (Acts 4:29). Then, in answer to their prayer, the
Spirit of God subsequently comes upon them, manifesting similar
effects: '... and they were all filled with the Holy Spirit, and
began to speak the word of God with *boldness* ' (Acts 4:31).
Paul exhorts the Ephesians to pray because he seeks this Spirit-
produced experience in his preaching: 'and pray on my behalf,
that utterance may be given to me in opening my mouth, to make
known with *boldness* the mystery of the gospel' (Eph. 6:19). In
each of these instances the same word is used, παρρησία. It
means 'outspokenness, frankness ... that conceals nothing and
passes over nothing ... confidence, boldness, fearlessness,
especially in the presence of persons of high rank'.[8] Hahn asserts
that this word 'is not a human quality; it comes from God ... it
characterizes effective preaching .... It is the fruit of the Holy
Spirit that has to be sought again and again.'[9]

When the Holy Spirit powerfully attends the preaching of the
word of God there is an ease of speaking, a holy authority, an

other-worldly kind of courage that can compel an ordinary man to invade the domain of darkness and demand the deliverance of people enslaved to that realm. Lloyd-Jones says:

> I like to put it like this – and I know of nothing on earth that is comparable to this feeling – that when this happens you have a feeling that you are not actually doing the preaching, you are looking on. You are looking on at yourself in amazement as this is happening. It is not your effort; you are just the instrument, the channel, the vehicle: and the Spirit is using you, and you are looking on in great enjoyment and astonishment. There is nothing that is in any way comparable to this.[10]

Spurgeon speaks in similar terms:

> If I were forbidden to enter heaven, but were permitted to select my state for all eternity, I should choose to be as I sometimes feel in preaching the gospel. Heaven is foreshadowed in such a state: the mind shut out from all disturbing influences, adoring the majestic and consciously present God, every faculty aroused and joyously excited to its utmost capability, all the thoughts and powers of the soul joyously occupied in contemplating the glory of the Lord, and extolling to listening crowds the Beloved of our soul; and all the while the purest conceivable benevolence towards one's fellow creatures urging the heart to plead with them on God's behalf—what state of mind can rival this?[11]

There are occasions when descriptions such as these truly reflect the experience of the God-sent preacher. In a manner of speaking he can say, *à la* Eric Liddel, 'When I preach I *feel* His pleasure.' However, it is also important to acknowledge that there are occasions when, to the preacher, the presence and power of the Spirit of God seem absent in any sensible way. Distraction rules his mind. Words come sluggishly. Passion seems forced. It is not uncommon for the gospel preacher to feel as though he has failed miserably in his attempt to deliver the word of God. On not a few Sunday afternoons I have been filled with such deep personal disappointment I have declared to my wife that I will never preach again. One seasoned preacher has said aptly:

The pulpit calls those anointed to it as the sea calls it sailors, and like the sea it batters and bruises and does not rest. To preach, to really preach, is to die naked a little at a time, and to know each time you do it that you must do it again.[12]

To be sure, there will be Sundays when the man of God will have no sense of the operation of the Holy Spirit in his preaching. Nevertheless, he must learn that any lack of the Spirit's 'felt presence' on his part is not the infallible barometer of divine work among the congregation. When I have been least aware of the Spirit's enablement, I have often received telephone calls or letters from parishioners giving testimony to some significant effect of the Spirit's work through the preaching.[13] This supplies me with a necessary reminder that preaching itself, properly speaking, is not efficacious. 'There is no *ex opere operato* (*i.e.,* it works automatically because of its sacramental power) in preaching.'[14] Rather, efficacy in preaching can only be attributed to a sovereign work of the Spirit, which, at times, may be altogether indistinguishable to the preacher himself. In most instances, the congregation will be the most astute witness to the manifest power of the Holy Spirit in preaching. Miller states: 'When the Holy Spirit invades our sermons, the other world looms almost visible as the flock is inflamed with intrigue.'[15] Hearers will be moved. Hearers will be gripped. Hearers will be humbled. Hearers will be comforted. Some hearers may even be angered.[16] Such are but some of the effects of the vitality of the Spirit.

Having come this far, it is imperative that we do not overlook a related fact of significant importance. It must be remembered that this power related to preaching is not an impersonal force floating about the cosmos. Rather, it is the property of a Person, a Divine Person who dispenses it according to His own good pleasure and eternal purpose. As such, it can never be programed or packaged. It cannot be coerced or manipulated. It is not available on demand. The vitality of the Spirit is not another sure-fire methodology for church growth packaged in Reformed piety. 'The wind blows where it wishes' (John 3:8), Jesus told Nicodemus.

In other words, the Spirit of God is sovereign. Consequently, His effects are manifested sovereignly.

The ramifications of these two truths should be obvious to those of us who are preachers. It means that we must live with the painful possibility that the results produced by the Spirit may not be satisfying to us. Here, again, is the occupational vulnerability of preaching. It is to be possessed by a holy compulsion but hobbled by human inability. To be sure, there will be continuous pain for the man called to this task. Everything in his native constitution will seek to escape it. *But he must not seek to elude the pain by redefining the aim.* The dilemma in which he finds himself reflects a genius of a supernatural kind. It forces him to seek his adequacy outside of himself:

> And my message and my preaching were not in persuasive words of wisdom, but in demonstration of the Spirit and of power, that your faith should not rest on the wisdom of men, but on the power of God (1 Cor. 2:4-5).

As C. H. Spurgeon put it:

> The gospel is preached in the ears of all; it only comes with power to some. The power that is in the gospel does not lie in the eloquence of the preacher; otherwise men would be converters of souls. Nor does it lie in the preacher's learning; otherwise it would consist in the wisdom of men. We might preach till our tongues rotted, till we should exhaust our lungs and die, but never a soul would be converted unless there were mysterious power going with it – the Holy Ghost changing the will of man. O Sirs! we might as well preach to stone walls as to preach to humanity unless the Holy Ghost be with the word, to give it power to convert the soul.[17]

Notes
   1. Henry C. Fish, *Power in the Pulpit* (Carlisle: Banner of Truth Trust, n.d.), pp. 1-2.
   2. E. M. Bounds, *Power Through Prayer* (repr. ed., Grand Rapids: Baker Book House, 1972), pp. 95-98.
   3. Archibald Robertson and Alfred Plummer, *The First Epistle of St. Paul to the Corinthians* (repr. ed., Edinburgh: T & T Clark, 1994), p. 34.
   4. Donald G. Bloesch, *God the Almighty* (Downers Grove: InterVarsity Press, 1995), p. 70.
   5. _____, *Essentials of Evangelical Theology* (San Francisco: HarperCollins Publishers, 1978), vol. 2, pp. 94-95.
   6. The prepositional phrases 'ἐν σοφίᾳ ... ἐν δυνάμει θεοῦ' are difficult to translate. Some suggest that the dative prepositions should be taken in a locatival sense, *i.e.* 'in the sphere of man's wisdom ... in the sphere of God's power.' Robertson and Plummer, *Corinthians*, p. 34. Others conclude that the two uses of ἐν are better translated 'on'. Simon Kistemaker, *Exposition of the First Epistle to the Corinthians* (Grand Rapids: Baker Book House, 1993), p. 78. A third option is to take ἐν in a casual or instrumental sense, thus rendering it 'because of' or 'by means of'. Turner asserts that Paul employs this sense of ἐν on twenty-eight occasions in 1 Corinthians alone, including its usage here, Nigel Turner, 'Syntax,' *A Grammar of New Testament Greek*, ed. James Hope Moulton (Edinburgh: T & T Clark, 1963), vol. 3, pp. 252-253. To be sure, grammarians indicate that there is often a 'blending' or 'fluctuation' between the locative and the instrumental use of ἐν, A. T. Robertson, *A Grammar of the Greek New Testament in the Light of Historical Research* (Nashville: Broadman Press, 1934), p. 590 and F. Blass and A. Debrunner, *A Greek Grammar of the New Testament* (Chicago: The University of Chicago Press, 1961), p. 118. Hence, the cautious assessment should be heeded: 'In simple truth the only way to know the resultant meaning of ἐν is to note carefully the context', Robertson, *Grammar*, p. 589. In the opinion of this author the casual sense appears most appropriate to the context (cf. 1:4), *i.e.* 'so that your faith should not exist because of the wisdom of men but as a consequence of the power of God.'
   7. Charles Hodge, *A Commentary on 1 & 2 Corinthians* (repr. ed., Carlisle: The Banner of Truth Trust, 1994), p. 32.
   8. William F. Arndt and F. Wilbur Gingrich, *A Greek-English Lexicon of the New Testament and Other Early Christian Literature* (Chicago: The University of Chicago Press, 1979), p. 630.
   9. H. -C. Hahn, 'παρρησία', *The New International Dictionary of New Testament Theology,* ed. Colin Brown (Grand Rapids: Zondervan Publishing House, 1979), vol. 2, p. 736.
   10. D. Martyn Lloyd-Jones, *Preaching and Preachers* (Grand Rapids:

Zondervan Publishing Company, 1971), p. 324.

11. Charles Haddon Spurgeon, *Lectures to my Students* (repr. ed., Pasadena: Pilgrim Publications, 1990), pp. 8-9.

12. This quote was cited without reference in a tape-recorded sermon by Alistair Begg entitled, 'The Pulpit: Its Power and its Pitfalls.'

13. 'Sometimes I have noticed that a word cast in, by the way, has done more than all the rest of the sermon. Sometimes when I thought I had done the least, then it developed that the most has been accomplished; and at other times when I thought I had really gotten hold of them, I found I had fished for nothing', John Bunyan, *Grace Abounding to the Chief of Sinners* (repr. ed., Chicago: Moody Press, 1959), p. 100.

14. Bernard Ramm, *After Fundamentalism* (San Francisco: Harper and Row, Publishers, 1983), p. 53.

15. Calvin Miller, *Spirit, Word, and Story* (Dallas: Word Publishing, 1989), p. 19.

16. 'Even when men hear this preaching and find in it an occasion for stumbling and resisting the gospel, this word is not without effectiveness or power ... it accomplishes the unfathomable designs of God and never returns to him without effect .... The gospel accomplishes its work even in those who are lost. It is for them an occasion for falling, for offense, because they make a folly of it; a stumbling-block, a fragrance of death which leads to death (Luke 2:34; Rom. 9:32; 1 Cor. 1:23; 2 Cor. 2:16; 1 Pet. 2:8). The word of God is always and everywhere a power of God, a sword of the Spirit .... It is always effective in some way .... When it does not lift up, it casts down; when it is not an occasion for restoration, it is an occasion for falling; when it is not a fragrance of life, it is a fragrance of death. According to the unfathomable designs of God and with a complete freedom, the Spirit uses it to convert, but also to harden; to restore, but also to be a stone of stumbling and to break those who fall upon it (Matt. 21:44)', Pierre Ch. Marcel, *The Relevance of Preaching* (Grand Rapids: Baker Book House, 1963), pp. 15, 32-33.

17. Attributed to Charles Haddon Spurgeon without reference in John R. W. Stott, *Between Two Worlds: The Art of Preaching in the Twentieth Century* (Grand Rapids: William B. Eerdmans Publishing Company, 1982), p. 335.

8

PREACHING AND THE MAN OF GOD

The influence of the Holy Spirit comes not as a bounty
upon indolence, but as a stimulus to exertion.
JOHN ANGELL JAMES

Preaching, in one sense, merely discharges the firearm
that God has loaded in the silent place.
CALVIN MILLER

We can only erect the altar: it is Your prerogative to send the fire.
GEOFFREY THOMAS

The Sovereignty of the Spirit and Human Involvement

The group was singing earnestly, the drums were pounding, the guitarists were strumming away and the audience was tapping their feet – but the Spirit was not there. They sang songs for an hour, building up to a great crescendo and sitting down in an aura of well-being – but the Spirit was not there. The preacher gave his message, told his stories, made them laugh, and made them cry – but the Spirit was not there. He began his appeal and worked them over, some needed to come to the front to be saved, others to rededicate their lives, others for inner healing, others to talk to counselors about their problems. A crowd gathered. A man said to himself, 'I want to be happy like these people,' and he went forward – but the Spirit was not there. After the service was over the people talked to one another about their activities and plans, and nobody realized that again the Spirit was not in their midst.

Down the road in another church the pastor announced the hymns of Toplady and Watts and a metrical Psalm, and the congregation sang – but the Spirit was not there. *The New International Version* was read – but the Spirit was not there. The preacher prayed for the congregation and the community; he thanked God for the gospel – but the Spirit was not there. Afterwards the congregation quietly went home, as aware as the minister had been that things were not as they should be, nor as they could be in the church of the living God.

When the blessing of God is removed from a gospel church which is worshipping in the old ways, the results are immediate and pathetic. If the Spirit of God is not inhabiting the praise of the people and the proclamation of the preacher, there is nothing left but bare walls. However, when the Spirit is driven out of a church which has handclapping, 'loadsachoruses', a band, racy sermons, laughter and altar calls, it will be about a millennium or two before anyone notices that He has gone – because even when He is not there they act as if He were, the atmosphere feels 'religious'.

One day the preacher fell before God and cried, 'Lord, I cannot go on without Your blessing. David said of you, "He restoreth my soul." My soul stands in need of restoration. I seem to do everything like a religious robot without even thinking of You or invoking Your aid' – and the Spirit began to move.

The preacher searched the Bible, asking what are the marks of the Spirit's presence? He learned that defiant sin in his own life or blatant sin tolerated in the congregation quenches the Spirit. If he misrepresented God and His way of salvation or if he fellowshipped with the ungodly, he found that that would grieve God the Spirit. He discovered that if he boldly preached on sin and righteousness and judgment that the Spirit Himself came in his preaching and testified of these sober realities. Most important of all, if he glorified the Lord Jesus Christ and spoke much of Him as God the Son, and the Savior of all who trust in Him, then that work which the Spirit most delightfully assisted and blessed was apparent. The great lesson he learned, as if for the first time, was that the Spirit is given to those who obey God. He sought painfully to change his ways, discipline his life, be more resolute in studying the word of God, spending longer in the presence of the Savior, avoiding those patterns of life that left him morose before the television to the neglect of his family. He went out after people who had been long on the fringes of the church and talked to them about their need of Christ. He gave more time to preparing his sermons, thinking of the people he was preaching to and the God in whose presence he stood when he spoke His word. He continually acknowledged his own need of the Spirit – 'Without You I can do nothing!'

On Sunday he stood before his congregation and prayed, 'Lord, we fear going through this service hearing the voice of men – our own singing of hymns, and the preacher's speaking the word. We dread the thought that we will leave this building in an hour and not have known the fellowship and secret sovereign testimony of Your Holy Spirit to our hearts. We confess our sins to You; we cry out in our helplessness and in our need of You. Come and have mercy upon us. We can only erect an altar: it is Your prerogative to send the fire.'

Then the forgiving Spirit, long-grieved, modestly returned and breathed upon them all. 'If anyone hears My voice and opens the door, I will come in and eat with him, and he with Me' (Rev. 3:20).[1]

But the Spirit was not there. No statement concerning a local church could be any more disconcerting. No statement could arouse any greater depth of fear in the heart of the man of God. How would a pastor respond if, amidst the typically-asked questions, the following was posed to him by a prospective visitor during an inquiring telephone conversation:

Inquirer: 'Do you have activities for young people at your church?'
Pastor: 'Every month.'
Inquirer: 'Does your worship service include contemporary music?'
Pastor: 'By all means.'
Inquirer: 'Do you preach from the Bible?'
Pastor: 'We most certainly do.'
Inquirer: 'Does your church sponsor home Bible studies?'
Pastor: 'Yes, in various locations and including diverse topics.'
Inquirer: 'Is there a mid-week prayer meeting at your church?'
Pastor: 'Wednesdays at 7:00pm. All are welcome.'
Inquirer: *'But, may I ask, is the Spirit present in your meetings?'*

Some may regard this question as an expression of ignorance. Others may regard it as a display of impudence. 'Of course, the Holy Spirit is present in our meetings,' one might retort. 'After all, as the fully divine, third-person of the Godhead, He is omnipresent.' In fidelity to biblical revelation, all Christians should readily confess the omnipresence of the Holy Spirit; specifically, that He is everywhere present with the totality of His being. David asks: 'Where can I go from Thy Spirit? Or where can I flee from Thy presence' (Ps. 139:7). The words which follow emphatically affirm his conviction that escape from the omnipresent Spirit is impossible. Yet, with similar emphasis, it is necessary for evangelicals to acknowledge that the *immediacy* of the Spirit's presence can, and does, vary. To say it differently, the omnipresence of the Holy Spirit is not synonymous with the *effects* or *influences* of the Spirit; what Christians from previous generations have termed 'the manifest presence of the Spirit', 'the sensible presence of the Spirit', or 'the felt presence of the Spirit'. To be sure, the omnipresence of the Holy Spirit is a fact that Christians can always assume. Being fully divine, He is always present. In contrast, the effects of His presence can never be presupposed. That is to say, they can be graciously given. They can also be judiciously withdrawn.

Moreover, the manifestations of His power are in keeping with His sovereign purpose and pleasure. Though gospel preachers are altogether dependent upon Him for the work of salvation and sanctification, the Holy Spirit can never be domesticated to perform on demand. He is not a servant poised at the ready, listening for the beckon call of preachers. He cannot be controlled. He cannot be manipulated against His will. His effects cannot be programmed. He is the Lord. But this raises a question of significant importance: since the Spirit of God is sovereign in His operations, does it naturally follow that both preacher and congregation are exempt from any responsibility in the work of salvation and sanctification? Does the Lordship of the Spirit alleviate our participation in this endeavor? The answer must be a resounding 'no'. Biblical Christians must never allow fatalism to exist as a caricature of divine sovereignty. In reality, predestination does not undercut human involvement. It demands it. The God who has ordained the end (the saving and sanctifying of sinners), has also ordained the means to achieve this end. *Hence, in the Spirit-inspired word, there are specific responsibilities assigned to the people of God that, when carried out in faithfulness, He is most inclined to bless.* Properly speaking, some of these responsibilities are specific to the congregation. Others are more pertinent to the man called to the task of preaching. For the remainder of this chapter our attention will be given to three responsibilities assigned to the gospel preacher himself.

One Half of a Man's Ministry

Though the blessing of the Spirit of God can never be coerced, it is imperative to identify the specific responsibilities given to the man who has been set apart to preach the gospel. These are divinely-appointed means that the Spirit is apt to employ. The first of these three (not in order of importance) becomes evident through a series of repeated statements made by Jesus Himself on the night before His death. To the original apostolic preachers He speaks of a specific 'ministerial responsibility'. Attending this thrice-mentioned responsibility is the promise of divine favor. This responsibility set forth by Jesus can be summarized as follows: *the preacher must devote himself to a consistent pattern of fervent intercession.*

Recall to mind a text to which we have already given some consideration: 'Truly, truly, I say to you, he who believes in Me, the works that I do shall he do also; and greater works than these shall he do ...' (John 14:12a). This is the aspiration of the Christian preacher: to be useful unto the end of advancing the gospel of Jesus Christ (*i.e.* 'the greater works'). However, when the exhilaration of the assignment fades in the light of the growing awareness of human limitation it must be asked: on what basis will the messengers of Jesus Christ accomplish the greater works? As has already been seen, Jesus answers this question: '... greater works than these shall he do; because I go to the Father' (John 14:12b). On the basis of His redemptive accomplishments, namely, His death and resurrection/ascension, the Holy Spirit

will be given to Christians, which, among other things, will result
in the realization of the greater works (cf. John 16:7-11). But is
it proper, then, to infer that the Holy Spirit will accomplish these
works irrespective of human involvement? Such an inference
would be a blatant disregard of the context at hand. Notice the
coordinating conjunction in the following words of Jesus: '*And*
whatever you ask in My name, that will I do, that the Father may
be glorified in the Son' (John 14:13). Carson states: 'The reason
why the "greater things" are done consequent upon Jesus' going
to the Father (v. 12) is now clarified further: the disciples' fruitful
conduct is the product of their prayers ...'[2] To be sure, the
indwelling and empowering Holy Spirit will be purchased by
the merits of Jesus Christ. But essential to the accomplishment of
the greater works is the prayer of these gospel ministers; that is,
prayer conditioned by the name of Jesus (*i.e.* not according to
the right incantation, but in harmony with all for which this name
stands), and to the ultimate end of the Father's glory.

Christians, at this very point, must resist the common temptation
to strip this verse from its context and thus lose the significance
of its meaning. Certainly, this is a prayer promise. But it is not a
universal prayer promise. Rather, it is a prayer promise in
relationship to the accomplishment of the greater works.
Moreover, the phrase 'that will I do' (John 14:13) is significant.
From it the disciples can derive two important implications:

(1) there will remain a *consistency* in these works. Scope,
not nature, is intended by the adjective 'greater'. In other words,
these 'greater works' will continue to be *His* works: 'the works
that I do shall he do also' (John 14:12);

and (2) there will remain a *continuity* in the source of their
accomplishment. Even though Jesus will have ascended to His
Father, it is *He* who will still be at work. The distinction of
verse 12 and verse 13, then, is not between the works of Jesus
and the greater works of His followers. Instead, it is between the
works that Jesus performed during the days of His public ministry
and those He now performs through His people.

The fundamental ground by which the greater works are made possible is the 'going' of Jesus to the Father, *i.e.*, his death and resurrection to sovereignty which releases the powers of the kingdom of God in the world; the second ground is the prayer of the disciples in the name of Jesus, *i.e.* prayer with appeal to his name, in response to which *the risen Lord himself will do what is asked*. The continuity of thought demands that the prayer that is made is in relation to the disciples' ministry, and the Lord on high will through His disciples perform the greater works. The contrast accordingly is not between Jesus and His disciples in their respective ministries, but between Jesus with His disciples in the limited circumstances of His earthly ministry and the risen Christ with His disciples in the post-Easter situation. Then the limitations of the Incarnation will no longer apply, redemption will have been won for the world, the kingdom of God opened for humanity, and the disciples equipped for a ministry in power to the nations.[3]

The promise of Jesus is that the greater works will be achieved by virtue of His redemptive accomplishments *and* the praying of those He is sending out to proclaim the gospel.

Jesus further illustrates the significance of prayer in the subsequent chapter: 'If you abide in Me, and My words abide in you, ask whatever you wish, and it shall be done for you' (John 15:7). Again, this prayer promise must not be extricated from its context. The overall theme of verses 1-8 is spiritual productivity (certainly including the work of salvation and sanctification), conveyed beautifully in the imagery of fruitbearing. In verse 1 Jesus speaks of the vine and the vinedresser. In verse 2 He elaborates on the work of the vinedresser. Verse 3 records Jesus' assurance that the disciples were already clean branches. In verse 4 the disciples are exhorted to abide in the vine in order to be spiritually productive. Jesus promises abundant fruitbearing in verse 5. Verse 6 speaks of the fate of fruitless branches. What, then, is discovered in verse 7? Not a disrelated, generically universal prayer promise, followed then by a resumption of Jesus' discussion on fruitbearing in verse 8. Rather, verse 7 supplies a description of the way fruitbearing occurs; *i.e.* by the means of answered prayer. More specifically, when the man of God abides in Christ (when he earnestly cultivates his intimate communion with the Vine), and when the word of Christ abides in him (when the word of Christ is the predominating influence in his life), he will prove effective in prayer because he will pray in keeping with the design of God; more specifically, for those concerns related to fruitbearing.

Later in the same chapter, with even greater emphasis, Jesus establishes prayer as the principle means of success in gospel ministry: 'You did not choose Me, but I chose you, and appointed you, that you should go and bear fruit, and that your fruit should remain, that whatever you ask of the Father in My name, He may give to you' (John 15:16). Three observations can be made regarding the prayer promise at the end of this verse: (1) it is a promise conditioned by the name of Jesus Christ; (2) it is a promise that assures the answer of the Father (not the impersonal, 'it will be given to you,' but instead, 'He may give to you'); and, (3) it is a promise made in relationship to fruitbearing. It is evident that the fruit about which Jesus here speaks is specifically the fruit of conversions; that which is the product of a divine appointment and commission ('I appointed you, that you should *go* and bear fruit').

Throughout the Upper Room discourse Jesus is exceedingly consistent: prayer is to be the preoccupation of the man sent out to proclaim the message of the gospel. Whether the consideration at hand is the accomplishment of greater works or the production of spiritual fruit, the preacher must devote himself to a consistent pattern of fervent intercession. The confession of the apostles was as follows: '*we will devote ourselves to prayer,* and to the ministry of the word' (Acts 6:4a). About this text Bridges has rightfully said: 'Prayer ... is one half of a man's ministry; and it gives to the other half all its power and success.'[4] He continues:

> Without prayer, a Minister is of no use to the church, nor of any advantage to mankind. He sows; and God gives no increase. He preaches; and his words are only like 'sounding brass, or a tinkling

cymbal'. He recites the praises of God; while 'his heart is far from Him'. It is prayer alone, then, that gives the whole strength and efficacy to our different administrations: and that man ceases, if I may use the expression, to be a public Minister from the time he ceases to pray.[5]

Calvin Miller concurs:

> The oral side of our career is visible, but it is never the source of spiritual power. In fact, our devotional life ... is the secret of real clout. A friend of mine long ago reminded me that I could not help people if I was always with people .... When Harold Fickett, Jr., says, 'A preacher is the epic poet of his people,' we must admit that the epic gains its form from silence .... Preaching from the silent center is the evidence that we who preach on trust are also living it. Preaching, in one sense, merely discharges the firearm that God has loaded in the silent place. The successful volley does not mean that we have passed homiletics but rather that we have been with God.[6]

Finally, the words of Edward Payson summarize aptly the indispensability of prayer for the preacher of the gospel: 'It is in the *closet* that the battle is lost or won.'[7]

First and foremost, preachers should be men of prayer. If, with any kind of integrity, the man of God is to pray for the vitality of the Spirit, then he must guard his devotional life against all intruders. For this reason, barring emergencies, I do not schedule appointments or receive telephone calls before 1:00pm. Like all hard-working pastors, if I pray only when people and circumstances allow it to be convenient, I would rarely pray. To be sure, this kind of priority can arouse accusations such as the following: 'Our pastor is unapproachable. It is difficult to get close to him. He is not very accessible.' Over time, however, maturing Christians will come to appreciate the value of such discipline. They themselves will be the benefactors of it. Until such a time, a preacher must rest in the conviction that the protection and cultivation of his own inner life is in the best interest of the congregation.

The man of God must give himself to prayer generally. More particularly, he should beseech God for the effects of the Holy Spirit through the instrumentality of his preaching. He should give God no rest, but incessantly make appeal to the throne of grace for the Spirit-produced work of conversion. He should continuously petition the Father for the sanctifying effects of the Spirit on behalf of the people entrusted to his care. A holy resolution should dominate the praying of the man called to preach: to seek the vitality of the Spirit for what it is, the premier element indispensable to any effectual preaching. Related to this concern, James Henley Thornwell has been noted for his passionate pleas to preachers of the gospel:

> ... of much greater importance than fine use of language was his fervent exhortation to all true gospel preachers to never be perfunctory in their preaching; never to go through the motions merely out of duty or desire to avoid shame. Rather, he urged them constantly to seek the illumination of the Holy Spirit, his unction, his blessing, and – as was so amply illustrated by the sermons of this master preacher himself – *to seek the fire of the altar to fall on the offering of their preaching.*[8]

The Great Instrument

A second responsibility is given to a preacher of the gospel: *he must prepare himself by the means of the diligent study of the scriptures.* As has been previously mentioned, the apostles were resolutely devoted to persevering in prayer. They also possessed an unrelenting commitment to 'the ministry of the word' (Acts 6:4). In a familiar passage Paul writes:

> 'You, however, continue in the things you have learned and become convinced of, knowing from whom you have learned them; and that from childhood you have known the sacred writings which are able to give you the wisdom that leads to salvation through faith which is in Christ Jesus. All scripture is inspired by God and profitable for teaching, for reproof, for correction, for training in righteousness; that the man of God may be adequate, equipped for every good work' (2 Tim. 3:14-17).

To be sure, this text does have secondary application to all believers. The God-breathed scriptures are for every Christian. But it must be remembered that the original intent of these words was directed from one preacher to another; from the Apostle Paul to Timothy. Moreover, Paul here uses the phrase 'man of God' in reference to Timothy, not merely as a Christian, but as a spiritual leader,[9] the pastor of the church in Ephesus (cf. 1 Tim. 6:11). In contrast to the deceptive and distorted voices surrounding Timothy, Paul commends the scriptures as the all-sufficient tool to render him adequate for the pastoral work to which God had called him: for teaching, reproof, correction, training in righteousness' (2 Tim. 3:16). The scriptures will equip the man of God for every good work. Succinctly, Vinet writes: 'The word is the pastor's great instrument.'[10]

Why bother with such an obvious principle? Often, in the context of discussions regarding the role of the Holy Spirit in preaching, many have concluded that diligent exegetical and theological Bible study is unnecessary. At one time or another most Christians have heard the following sentiments from a supposedly 'Spirit-filled' preacher: 'I don't prepare a sermon. I don't do the work of exegesis. I just trust God and pray. He gives me the words to say at each moment.' But at this point a clear distinction needs to be made. On the one hand, the Christian must affirm the Spirit's work of *illumination* (the opening of the mind to understand the meaning of the scriptures). On the other hand, the Christian is given no warrant for embracing *illuminism* (the tendency toward passivity and non-effort in the name of relying upon the Spirit). Christian preachers must never assume that a mutually exclusive decision needs to be made between pain-staking exegesis and reliance upon the Spirit. The issue for the preacher is not study *or* the Spirit, as though a wedge can be driven between the two. It is study *and* the Spirit. To be sure, study without prayer is atheism. It is a denial of the need of the Spirit's intervention for spiritual understanding. But prayer without study is presumption. It is the resting of confidence upon a hope never given by God.

The maxim of practical religion applies in full force to our subject. Labour in the preparation for the pulpit, as if our whole success depended on it. Pray, and depend wholly upon Christ; as feeling, that 'without him we can do nothing'. In neglecting preparation we tempt God to depart from his ordinary course; in trusting to our preparation, we make a God of our gifts .... We are warranted to expect assistance to the utmost extent of our necessity; and we must lay our whole stress upon it as the only source of *effective* meditation, composition, or delivery. But such a dependence as supersedes the necessity of preparation, is unscriptural and delusive.[11]

Paul's exhortation to Timothy needs to be heard afresh by gospel preachers: 'Be diligent to present yourself approved to God as a workman who does not need to be ashamed, handling accurately the word of truth' (2 Tim. 2:15). The verb, $\sigma\pi o\upsilon\delta\acute{a}\zeta\omega$, is a strong word meaning 'to be eager to do something, with the implication of readiness to expend energy and effort ... to do something with intense effort and motivation ...'[12] To be sure, the word of God is the Spirit's sword (Eph. 6:17), the instrument of revealing the mind of God and effecting the purposes of God. But preachers must not sheath this sword in the scabbard of their own laziness. Baxter states:

... if we give to reason, memory, study, books, methods, forms, &c., but their proper place in subordination to Christ and His Spirit, they are so far from being quenchers of the Spirit, that they are necessary in their places, and such means as we must use, if ever we will expect the Spirit's help.[13]

The gospel preacher can take great confidence in the fact that the Spirit of God speaks effectually through His rightly divided word.

Power Through Weakness

In a vestry in Aberdeen these words were used to confront the preacher ere he mounted the pulpit stairs: 'No man can glorify Christ and himself at the same time.' If the Holy Spirit is to speak through the preacher and the preaching he must have clear passage – not through a void, but through a mind and personality laid open in all its delicate and intrinsic parts to the operation of the Spirit, to the end that his total powers may be willingly and intelligently bent to the present purpose of God.[14]

What is the requisite of such dedication? A man must recognize the significance of his inabilities. All that has been thus far set forth in terms of prayer and exegetical diligence grows out of one all-encompassing recognition: any attempt to proclaim the word of God will prove futile if the only strength in which to do so is less than divine. A major step toward experiencing the power of God necessitates a thorough-going recognition of our lack of it. Herein, then, is the third responsibility given to the man of God: *the preacher must recognize, and even revel in, his own human inabilities.*

Of the many paradoxes that appear in Paul's Corinthian correspondences, one of the most significant is his recurring theme of power through weakness. Certainly this emphasis is taken because of the triumphalistic spirit so prevalent in Corinth. Such self-confidence invalidates the need for divine power and thus compromises the success of the gospel. Hence, Paul sets forth this apparent paradox on at least three occasions.[15] The reader should take note of three similar phrases ($\H{\iota}\nu\alpha$, or purpose clauses, translated 'that') which magnify the power-through-weakness motif. Consider the first:

And I was with you in weakness and in fear and in much trembling. And my message and my preaching were not in persuasive words of wisdom, but in demonstration of the Spirit and of power, *that* your faith should not rest on the wisdom of men, but on the power of God (1 Cor. 2:3-5).

Stated simply, Paul's conscious weakness gave way for the faith of the Corinthians to come into existence by the means of God's power. A second, and similar, phrase appears in 2 Corinthians 4: 'But we have this treasure in earthen vessels' (2 Cor. 4:7a). The message of the gospel, given to Paul and his associates, existed in frail, limited, and weak physical bodies. Paul elaborates:

> we are afflicted in every way, but not crushed; perplexed, but not despairing; persecuted, but not forsaken; struck down, but not destroyed; always carrying about in the body the dying of Jesus ... (2 Cor. 4:8-10).

What purpose did this serve? '... *that* the surpassing greatness of the power may be of God and not from ourselves' (2 Cor. 4:7b). Paul's evident weakness served to magnify the greatness of God's power. Finally, Paul raises this paradox again in 2 Corinthians 12:

> And because of the surpassing greatness of the revelations, for this reason, to keep me from exalting myself, there was given me a thorn in the flesh, a messenger of Satan to buffet me – to keep me from exalting myself! Concerning this I entreated the Lord three times that it might depart from me. And He has said to me, 'My grace is sufficient for you, for My power is perfected in weakness.' Most gladly, therefore, I will rather boast about my weaknesses, *that* the power of Christ may dwell in me. Therefore I am well content with weaknesses, with insults, with distresses, with persecutions, with difficulties, for Christ's sake; for when I am weak, then I am strong (2 Cor. 12:7-10).

If human weakness is the channel through which God most readily communicates His power, Paul was prepared not only to affirm his weakness, but to revel in it. Hence, his steady theme is undeniably evident: God's power is expressed through human weakness.

But, it may be asked, is this theme unique to Paul? One may answer 'yes' if the perspective from which this is being asked concerns the specific *explanation* of this power-through-weakness concept. However, without hesitation one must answer 'no' if the perspective from which this is being asked concerns the *record* of God's dealings with His spokesmen. That is to say, the Bible records the similar experiences of men like Joseph,

Moses, David, Elijah, Jeremiah and Hosea. The fact is, it is highly unlikely that any man will ever know of the Spirit's power until he is willing to confess before God, 'If You must hurt me to make me a suitable channel of Your power, then do so.' Sometimes this pain may be visible to the naked eye. On other occasions it may be hidden from public view. But this is God's most frequently employed means of equipping His servants. Hudson Taylor once stated: 'All God's giants have been weak men.'[16] Why is this the case? Because a weak man possesses no confidence in his own strength. When desperate for power he searches outside of himself.

Christian preachers are notorious for touting the successes of Charles Haddon Spurgeon (I will do so in the final chapter!). Unfortunately, few are aware of the weaknesses that providence inflicted upon him. Spurgeon was a man who experienced deep bouts of depression for extended periods. In 1858, at age twenty-four, depression struck him for the first time, and consequently afflicted him for the rest of his life. He confessed of occasions when he 'could weep by the hour'.[17] When his wife Susannah was thirty-three years old she became a virtual invalid and rarely heard Spurgeon preach for the last twenty-seven years of his ministry. Spurgeon suffered from gout, rheumatism, and Bright's disease (inflammation of the kidneys). In fact, 'one third of the last twenty-two years of his ministry was spent out of the pulpit, either suffering, convalescing, or taking precautions against the return of these illnesses'.[18] In addition, Spurgeon endured a lifetime of public ridicule and slander. Occasionally, it was directed at him from unbelievers. Often, the source of the attack came from other preachers.[19] How, it must be asked, did Spurgeon himself interpret these manifold experiences of suffering and affliction:

Instruments shall be used, but their intrinsic weakness shall be clearly manifested; there shall be no division of the glory, no diminishing of the honor due the Great Worker. The man shall be emptied of self, and then filled with the Holy Ghost .... My witness is, that those who are honored of their Lord in public, have usually to endure a secret chastening, or to carry a peculiar cross, lest by any means they exalt themselves, and fall into the snare of the devil .... Such humbling but salutary messages our depressions whisper in our ears; they tell us in a manner not to be mistaken that we are but men, frail, feeble, apt to faint.[20]

God will have no competitors. For this reason He manifests His power through weakness. It is, therefore, incumbent upon the gospel preacher to recognize the overpowering nature of his inabilities; to be able to say with Paul: 'who is adequate for these things?' (2 Cor. 2:16). 'The strength of the pulpit is in its own conscious weakness, and in God's almighty power.'[21]

Many years ago a famous violinist died. Leaving behind no family members, there was no one to whom he could bequeath his Stradivarius. An auction was summarily convened, in part, to sell the instrument. It was eventually purchased by another violinist. He paid twenty thousand dollars for the violin, a sizeable sum in its day.

Shortly thereafter the new owner of the Stradivarius announced that he would play a concert on his new violin. When the evening arrived the concert hall was filled to capacity. People were waiting in breathless anticipation. At just the right moment he walked out on stage with nothing but his violin and he began to play a composition of Paganini. He held the audience spell-bound. His technique was flawless. His tone was exquisite. At the conclusion of the final note, the audience instantaneously jumped to their feet and roared with applause. He bowed, simply, and walked off stage. A few seconds later, with the applause still thundering, he walked back on stage, took his violin by its neck, raised it over his head and smashed it on a nearby piano bench, shattering it into a thousand pieces. He then walked off the stage. The audience was horrified. They were stunned. A moment later a second man walked out on stage and stood before the people. They became very quiet as he spoke these words: 'The violin on which the maestro has just performed his first selection, the same violin that he has just destroyed, was but a twenty dollar violin. He will now perform the rest of the concert on the twenty-thousand dollar Stradivarius.'

What was the point he was attempting to make? The genius is never in the violin. It is always in the violinist. And the same is true for the preacher. At best, he is but a twenty dollar violin. But music can be heard when he is taken up in the hands of the Heavenly Violinist.

We do not worship the rod of Moses, the trumpet of Gideon, or the slingshot of David. Such would be grievous expressions of misdirected worship. But such is also the case when the preacher rests his confidence in the power of his own abilities. 'What then is Apollos? And what is Paul? Servants through whom you believed, even as the Lord gave opportunity to each one' (1 Cor. 3:5). The man is nothing. God is everything.

Notes

1. Geoffrey Thomas, 'The Return of the Holy Spirit: A Modern Parable', *Reformation and Revival Journal,* ed., John Armstrong (Vol. III, No. 2, 1994), pp. 29-31.

2. D. A. Carson, *The Gospel According to John* (Grand Rapids: William B. Eerdmans Publishing Company, 1991), pp. 496-497.

3. George R. Beasley-Murray, *John* (Waco: Word Books, Publisher, 1987), p. 255.

4. Charles Bridges, *The Christian Ministry with an Inquiry into the Causes of its Inefficiency* (repr. ed., Carlisle: The Banner of Truth Trust, 1991), p. 148.

5. *Ibid.*, p. 147.

6. Calvin Miller, *Spirit, Word, and Story* (Dallas: Word Publishing, 1989), pp. 25-26.

7. This is attributed to Payson without reference in Henry C. Fish, *Power in the Pulpit* (Carlisle: The Banner of Truth Trust, n.d.), p. 19.

8. Douglas Kelly, *Preachers with Power: Four Stalwarts of the South* (Carlisle: The Banner of Truth Trust, 1992), p. 83.

9. 'ὁ ἄνθρωπος τοῦ θεοῦ ...' is used of the Christian standing in the service of God (1 Tim. 6:11; 2 Tim. 3:17); in the LXX of Moses (Deut. 33:1), David (2 Chr. 8:14). Joachim Jeremias, 'ἄνθρωπος,' *Theological Dictionary of the New Testament,* ed., Gerhard Kittel (Grand Rapids: William B. Eerdmans Publishing Company, 1964), vol. 1, p. 364.

10. A. Vinet, *Homiletics* (New York: Ivison and Phinney, 1854), p. 21.

11. Bridges, *Christian Ministry,* p. 221.

12. Johannes P. Louw and Eugene A. Nida, *Greek-English Lexicon of the New Testament Based on Semantic Domains* (New York: United Bible Societies, 1989), vol. 1, pp. 298, 662.

13. Richard Baxter, *Practical Works* (repr. ed., Ligonier: Soli Deo Gloria Publications, 1990), vol. 4, p. 567.

14. William Still, 'The Holy Spirit in Preaching,' *Christianity Today* (Sept. 2, 1957), p. 9.

15. For this idea I am indebted to John R. W. Stott, *Between Two Worlds: The Art of Preaching in the 20th Century* (Grand Rapids: William B. Erdmans Publishing Company, 1982), pp. 330-332.

16. This quote attributed to Taylor is cited without reference in Stott, *Between Two Worlds,* p. 332.

17. Darrel W. Amundsen, 'The Anguish and Agonies of Charles Spurgeon', *Christian History* (Volume X, No. 1), p. 24.

18. Iain H. Murray, ed., *Letters of Charles Haddon Spurgeon* (Carlisle: The Banner of Truth Trust, 1992), p. 116.

19. Joseph Parker wrote: 'Mr. Spurgeon was absolutely destitute of intellectual benevolence. If men saw as he did they were orthodox; if they saw things in some other way they were heterodox, pestilent and unfit to lead the minds of students or inquirers. Mr. Spurgeon's was a superlative egotism; not the shilly-shallying, timid, half-disguised egotism that cuts off its own head, but the full-grown, over-powering, sublime egotism that takes the chief seat as if by right.' Cited in Erroll Hulse and David Kingdon, eds., *A Marvelous Ministry: How the All-Round Ministry of Charles Haddon Spurgeon Speaks to us Today* (Pittsburgh: Soli Deo Gloria Publications, 1993), p. 128. James Wells, the hyper-Calvinist, wrote of Spurgeon: 'I have – most certainly have – my doubts as to the Divine reality of his conversion.' *Ibid.,* p. 35.

20. Charles Haddon Spurgeon, *Lectures to my Students* (repr. ed., Pasadena: Pilgrim Publications, 1990), pp. 177-178.

21. Gardiner Spring, *The Power of the Pulpit* (Carlisle: The Banner of Truth Trust, 1986), p. 81.

9

THE SENSITIVE SPIRIT

Our work is, no doubt, greatly affected, for good or evil,
by the condition of the congregation.
CHARLES HADDON SPURGEON

The congregation which is being awakened by the proclamation
of the word of God will demonstrate the genuineness of its
faith by honouring the office of preaching in its unique
glory and by serving it with all its powers.
DIETRICH BONHOEFER

Can we doubt that the present barrenness of the Church's
life is God's judgment on us for the way in which we
have dishonoured the Holy Spirit?
J. I. PACKER

Muted Trumpets

In the late 1580s a graduate of St. Andrews College arrived in
Edinburgh to fill a pastoral charge that, just twenty-five years
earlier, had been occupied by the great Scottish Reformer, John
Knox. The name of this young man was Robert Bruce, and his
ministry would prove to be a contributing factor to the spiritual
light for which Edinburgh was to become conspicuous. In
particular, his preaching at St. Giles Cathedral steadily bore
witness to a power that betrayed a heavenly origin. Robert Fleming
writes:

Whilst he was in the ministry at Edinburgh he shined as a great light
through the whole land, the power and efficacy of the Spirit most

sensibly accompanying the word he preached ... his speech and his preaching was in such evidence and demonstration of the Spirit that by the shining of his face, and that shower of divine influence, wherewith the word spoken was accompanied, it was easy for the hearer to perceive that he had been in the mount with God ... he preached ordinarily with such life and power, and the word spoken by him was accompanied with such a manifest presence, that it was evident to the hearers that he was not alone at the work ... some of the most stout-hearted of his hearers were ordinarily made to tremble, and by having these doors which formerly had been bolted against Jesus Christ, as by an irresistible power broke open, and the secrets of their hearts made manifest, they went away under convictions and carrying with them undeniable proofs of Christ speaking in him.[1]

Should not experiences such as these be the longing of every evangelical congregation? In anticipation of hearing the word preached, should not effects such as the aforementioned be the aspiration of the people of God? Each week Christians contend with the pressures of strained budgets, stressful jobs, sickly bodies, and fragile relationships. Consequently, more is needed on the Lord's Day than mere enthusiasms from a motivational speaker. More is needed than a fresh set of techniques from the latest pop-psychologist. It is the voice of the living Christ that people need to hear through the preaching of the evangelical scriptures; to sense the 'power and efficacy of the Spirit most sensibly accompanying the word'. The congregation needs to recognize a man 'not alone at the work' as he stands before them. To be sure, such a recognition is consequent upon the good pleasure of the sovereign Spirit. But this does not exempt the people of God from any and all responsibility in the matter.

The preacher himself must be a man of relentless prayer. He must give himself indefatigably to the study of the scriptures. He must recognize, and even revel in, his own obvious inabilities. In practical terms, the preacher gives himself to the ominous task of understanding a passage of scripture so that he might proclaim it to the eternal benefit of people who will gather on the Lord's

Day. He diligently labors in a text, seeking to understand the meaning of the words, their grammatical relationships, and their unique literary genre. He gives thoughtful consideration to the history, geography, and culture standing behind these words. He seeks to understand his text within the movement of the author's argument, keeping in mind the extending contexts of paragraphs, chapters, and the book itself. Finally, he seeks to identify the purpose of the passage as it is revealed in the history of redemption; *i.e.* how it foreshadows, establishes, builds upon, or reveals the need for the saving accomplishments of Jesus Christ.

Throughout this process the man of God prays. From beginning to end he asks for insight: 'Dear Spirit of truth, grant more illumination. I need more light. Make evident the meaning and relevance of Your word.' Then, as the meaning of the passage becomes clear, it begins to grip the heart of the preacher. To him it may now seem the most important passage in all of the Bible. Surely, the Holy Spirit has been operative. In the truest sense, however, the preacher still awaits a message from God. His prayers, therefore, take a new form: 'Unless Your Spirit attends my proclamation so as to effect the hearts of people, no one but me will benefit from the God-breathed word. I love these people. Their eternal well-being consumes me. They need a word from heaven.' Like unto Jacob of old, the preacher seeks to lay hold of God and say to Him: 'Until You bless me, I will not release You.' Perhaps one may question the indispensability, if not the value, of prayer if ample attention has been given to study and preparation. Yet it must be understood that unattended exegesis will not penetrate the human heart, accurate though it be. A polished manuscript will not transform. Hence, the preacher prays for the Spirit's vitality, His holy potency inhering the proclamation of the Christocentric word. More pointedly, he prays that the Spirit of God would attend his exposition of the scriptures with power *during the moment of proclamation*. Spurgeon has aptly captured this: 'Preachers sent from God are not musical boxes which, being once wound up, will play through their set tunes, but they are trumpets which are utterly mute until the living breath causes them to give forth a certain sound.'[2]

But at this point it should be asked: what are the responsibilities given to the *congregation* for the preaching of the word? It is safe to assume that most congregations (and their preachers!) would stand in amazement over this question. 'What do you mean the congregation has responsibility for the preaching?' a church member might ask. 'Of course, all believers have specific ministries for which they have been gifted. No Christian is exempt from service. But the preaching of the word is the job of the preacher. He has been called of God to this task. He has acquired a measure of education. He collects a salary from the church. Preaching is his work.' And yet, as I have been laboring to make clear: *the single most important ingredient in preaching is something the preacher himself cannot supply.* Adams exhorts: 'Too many laymen speak about the preaching event as if it were a one-way street, as if the responsibility for what transpires when the Bible is proclaimed rests solely on the shoulders of the preacher. But that's not so!'[3] Marcel adds:

> When, then, will the believers en masse understand that they are primarily responsible for the preaching which they hear, yes, more than their preachers ... preaching the word is a function and activity of the Church, not the function and specialty of a man.[4]

Do congregations give consideration to their relationship to Spirit-empowered preaching? More specifically, what are the responsibilities given to the congregation for the preaching of the word?

A Person Who Can Be Grieved

In the forefront of the congregation's consciousness should be two responsibilities related to the ministry of proclamation. As expressed in their original contexts, the first responsibility is implied from two specific passages, while the second is set forth in terms that are explicit. The first responsibility is set forth in terms that are remedial in emphasis, while the second is set forth in terms that are hortatory. For the remainder of this chapter consideration will be given to the first responsibility. The following chapter will take up the concern of the second. The first responsibility of the congregation may be summarized as follows: *the congregation must consciously refrain from any kind of attitude or activity that might contribute to a withholding of the effects of the Holy Spirit.*

Before any further development ensues, a theological presupposition must be identified as foundational to this argument; namely, that the Holy Spirit is a Person. In John 14:16 Jesus makes a vital promise to His men: 'And I will ask the Father, and He will give you another Helper.' The significance at this point lies in the substance of the promise: not *help* merely, but a *Helper;* not a reservoir from which to derive strength, but an accessible Person of inestimable power.[5] Jesus promises to His men a Helper, an Advocate, a Comforter. Furthermore, Jesus employs the masculine pronoun 'He' when making reference to the Holy Spirit (cf. John 14:26; 15:26; 16:7-8, 13-14). This is especially significant in 16:13 where the neuter pronoun 'it' would ordinarily be expected to match the neuter 'Spirit'.

Most Christians have no difficulty in grasping the personhood of God the Father. Of course, the term itself, 'Father', is an exceedingly personal term. Christians are encouraged to direct their prayers to the Father (Matt. 6:9), and are reminded that He watches over them (Matt. 10:29-30), loves them (Rom. 8:39), provides for them (Matt. 6:31-33), and even chastises them (Heb. 12:7-10). Christians would never refer to the Father by the neuter pronoun 'it'. The personhood of the Father is plainly evident. For many, it is even more natural to affirm the personhood of God the Son. He was the Babe at Bethlehem, the Carpenter of Nazareth, and the Savior of Golgotha. He is the risen Lord on the road to Emmaus and the ascended King reigning at the right hand of the Father. The Bible records the testimony of those who had cast their eyes upon Him, heard the sound of His voice, and even touched Him. Christians readily affirm the personhood of the Son.

Evangelicals are not so confident concerning the personhood of God the Spirit, however. Admittedly, the term 'Spirit' is less personal than the term 'Father'. Moreover, personhood is often associated with corporeality, and the Spirit has not become incarnate as has the Son. Nevertheless, the scriptures bear witness to the personhood of the Spirit by regarding Him as equal to both the Father and the Son, most notably in the Great Commission: 'Go therefore and make disciples of all the nations, baptizing them in the name of the Father and the Son and the Holy Spirit ...' (Matt. 28:19). If the Father and the Son are to be regarded as Persons, so too must the Holy Spirit be regarded as possessing full personhood. Furthermore, the scriptures indicate that the Holy Spirit performs actions that evidence personhood: He teaches (John 14:26), witnesses (John 15:26), convicts (John 16:8), guides (John 16:13), prays (Rom. 8:26-27), issues commands (Acts 8:29), calls ministers (Acts 13:2), appoints elders (Acts 20:28). These are works that, properly speaking, cannot be attributed to an impersonal source of power, but solely to a person. The Bible records certain actions that are performed in direct relationship to the Holy Spirit: He can be blasphemed (Matt. 12:31-32), lied to (Acts 5:3), resisted (Acts 7:51), obeyed (Acts 10:19-23), insulted (Heb. 10:29). These actions are performed in relationship to a person, not an impersonal force. Finally, the scriptures reveal manifestations of the Spirit's essence that are intrinsic to authentic personhood: He possesses a will (1 Cor. 12:11), intelligence (1 Cor. 2:11), and feelings. This leads us to the present concern; namely, that the Holy Spirit, as a person, can be grieved (cf. Isa. 63:10):

> Let no unwholesome word proceed from your mouth, but only such a word as is good for edification according to the need of the moment, that it may give grace to those who hear. And do not *grieve the Holy Spirit of God,* by whom you were sealed for the day of redemption (Eph. 4:29-30).

The verb $\lambda \upsilon \pi \acute{\epsilon} \omega$ means: 'to cause pain or grief ... to distress',[6] 'to cause someone to be sad, sorrowful, or distressed'.[7] To be even more exact, the construction of the verb demands the cessation of an action in progress: 'Stop grieving the Holy Spirit.' Paul employs anthropomorphic language to emphasize the Spirit's personhood.

To be sure, all sin is an offense against the holiness of God. It is noteworthy that Paul here cites the more complete name of the third Person of the Trinity: 'the *Holy* Spirit of God.' Paul's concern, however, is to inform Christians that sin not only offends God's holiness, it also wounds His love (cf. Rom. 15:30). Such sin on the part of His covenant people causes Him distress. But, it must be asked, why does Paul specifically identify the Holy Spirit as being grieved? His intention is not to exclude the First and Second Persons of the Godhead; rather, to spotlight the particular grief caused to the Spirit because of the unique category of sin being addressed. Like nothing else, sins of the tongue threaten the integrity of the fellowship. Gossip, evil speaking, criticism, lying, and slander, in a wickedly effectual way, endanger the unity of the Body of Christ, the establishment of which is the peculiar work of the Spirit (cf. Eph. 4:3). Certainly all sins bring grief to the Triune God. It must also be acknowledged, however, that sins of the tongue bring a singularly painful grief to the Holy Spirit because they directly threaten the unity He seeks to establish.

What, then, are the concerns pertinent to the subject at hand? Stated simply, the wounding of the Spirit can and often does, lead to a withdrawal of His influences. The well-known plea of David is illustrative at this point: 'do not take Thy Holy Spirit from me' (Ps. 51:11). Some have suggested that this plea is inappropriate for a new covenant believer. But such thinking reveals a failure to distinguish between the Spirit's *presence* in the Christian and the experience of His gracious *effects*.[8] John Stott explains: 'For the Holy Spirit is a sensitive Spirit. He hates sin, discord and falsehood, and shrinks away from them.'[9] Hodge adds:

His indwelling certifies that we are the children of God, and secures our final salvation .... To grieve him, therefore, is to wound him on whom our salvation depends. Though he will not finally withdraw from those in whom he dwells, yet when grieved he withholds the manifestations of his presence.[10]

By clear implication this addresses the congregation's responsibility for the effectiveness of the ministry of preaching. Sin among members of the fellowship, particularly sins of the tongue, grieves the holy sensibilities of the Spirit of God, thus compromising the effects of His divine influences. When Christians, by the means of sinful speaking, threaten the unity established by the Holy Spirit, they cut Him to the heart. Ultimately, this is to their own detriment because, in the division of labor that exists within the Godhead, the Holy Spirit is the immediate author of every blessing, every supernatural effect, every manifestation of grace. Only God knows what extent of blessing has been withheld because of grief caused to the sensitive Spirit. Spurgeon observes:

God the Spirit does not bless a collection of quarrelling professors. Those who are always contending, not for the truth, but for petty differences, and family jealousies, are not likely to bring to the church the dove-like Spirit. Want of unity always involves want of power.[11]

Congregations must consciously refrain from any kind of attitude or activity that might contribute to a withholding of the effects of the Holy Spirit. They must allow for nothing that would grieve Him. This, in part, is how the congregation contributes to the effectual proclaiming and hearing of the word of God.

A Fire That Can Be Extinguished
Paul sets forth a second negative exhortation which addresses the congregation's relationship to the Holy Spirit: 'Do not quench the Spirit' (1 Thess. 5:19). The word $\sigma\beta\acute{\epsilon}\nu\nu\upsilon\mu\iota$ means literally 'to put out a fire',[12] 'to extinguish by drowning with water'.[13]

Paul employs this word when developing the concept of spiritual warfare, specifically to *'extinguish* all the flaming missiles of the evil one' (Eph. 6:16). In the present text the figurative sense of σβέννυμι is intended 'to cause a fervent activity to cease',[14] to 'stifle, suppress'.[15] But to what is Paul referring? Some suggest that he has the gift of prophecy[16] in view (cf. 1 Thess. 5:20-22). However, in verse 19 Paul's concern appears to be more generic in emphasis, *i.e.* 'the Spirit' is not limited to one specific operation of the Holy Spirit (such as the gift of prophecy), but includes the whole range of the Spirit's gifts.[17] Best asserts:

> In verse 20 attention is directed to one particular gift, prophecy, but here the concern is more general: no gift of the Spirit is to be extinguished (*sbennyte*). The metaphor is especially vivid – the putting out of a flame or light – and is appropriate since 'fire' is associated with the Spirit (Matt. 3:11 = Luke 3:16; Acts 2:3f; 18:25; Rom. 12:11; 2 Tim. 1:6). If those who have been given gifts by the Spirit are either not allowed to exercise them within the community or what they say and do is ignored then the effect is that the fiery power and light of the Spirit is quenched and the church is not built up.[18]

Again, Paul uses a construction that demands the cessation of an activity in progress. In all probability, the Thessalonians were involved in a dispute that has manifested itself on many occasions. Thomas explains:

> ... it is evident that already in this assembly a tendency (exists) to discourage the use of some of the gifts. It appears that the undisciplined enthusiasm of some of the younger Christians in the use of their gifts had resulted in the abuse of them in the congregation. Because of this difficulty the more sober-minded leaders sought to guard against this disorder in the public meetings and had discouraged the exercise of gifts on the part of the less discreet. The writer would also speak in favor of order in congregational meetings (1 Cor. 14:40), but in this case he warns against the other extreme, that of squelching the gifts. As a result the assembly was cheated out of the benefits from them.[19]

Paul's exhortation is to the point: 'This must stop. No longer suppress the work of the Spirit among you. Welcome His gifts and the benefits that can be expressed through them.'

What is the forthcoming implication concerning the congregation's relationship to the preaching of the word? One predominant sensation should characterize God's people: active expectation. It is not enough for the congregation to possess a proper view of inspiration. They must gather on the Lord's Day expecting to hear the voice of God through the proclamation of the scriptures. They must bring an eagerness to hear, a readiness to submit, a predetermination to obey. Peter exhorts his readers to this end: 'like newborn babes, long for the pure milk of the word, that by it you may grow in respect to salvation' (1 Pet. 2:2). James writes: 'in humility receive the word implanted, which is able to save your souls' (Jas. 1:21). The eager expectation of Cornelius provides a fitting illustration: 'Now then, we are all here present before God to hear all that you have been commanded by the Lord' (Acts 10:33). Eugene Peterson captures this expectation by expressing the heart-felt, but often unspoken, desire of an authentic Christian congregation:

> We need help in keeping our beliefs sharp and accurate and intact. We don't trust ourselves; our emotions seduce us into infidelities. We know we are launched on a difficult and dangerous act of faith, and there are strong influences intent on diluting or destroying it. We want you to give us help. Be our pastor, a minister of word and sacrament in the middle of this world's life. Minister with word and sacrament in all the different parts and stages of our lives – in our work and play, with our children and our parents, at birth and death, in our celebrations and sorrows, on those days when morning breaks over us in a wash of sunshine, and those other days that are all drizzle. This isn't the only task in the life of faith, but it is your task. We will find someone else to do the other important and essential tasks. This is *yours*: word and sacrament.
>
> One more thing: We are going to ordain you to this ministry, and we want your vow that you will stick to it. This is not a temporary job assignment but a way of life that we need lived out in our

community. We know you are launched on the same difficult belief venture in the same dangerous world as we are. We know your emotions are as fickle as ours, and your mind is as tricky as ours. That is why we are going to *ordain* you and why we are going to exact a *vow* from you. We know there will be days and months, maybe even years, when we won't feel like believing anything and won't want to hear it from you. And we know there will be days and weeks and maybe even years when you won't feel like saying it. It doesn't matter. Do it. You are ordained to this ministry, vowed to it.

There may be times when we come to you as a committee or delegation and demand that you tell us something else than what we are telling you now. Promise right now that you won't give in to what we demand of you. You are not the minister of our changing desires, or our time-conditioned understanding of our needs, or our secularized hopes for something better. With these vows of ordination we are lashing you fast to the mast of word and sacrament so you will be unable to respond to the siren voices.

There are many other things to be done in this wrecked world, and we are going to be doing at least some of them, but if we don't know the foundational realities with which we are dealing – God, kingdom, gospel – we are going to end up living futile, fantasy lives. Your task is to keep telling the basic story, representing the presence of the Spirit, insisting on the priority of God, speaking the biblical words of command and promise and invitation.[20]

This is the contribution the preacher seeks from his congregation: a holy resolution to hear the word of the gospel both in and out of season. When the people of God gather with anticipation, possessed by a sincere desire to hear their Father's voice, preaching comes easily, almost as though the congregation draws it out of the preacher. Spurgeon says:

I have had great success in soul-winning ... but I have never taken any credit for it, for I feel that I preach under great advantages; the people come with an intense desire to hear, and with an expectation of getting a blessing .... When a congregation expects nothing, it generally finds nothing even in the best of preachers; but when they are prepared to make much of what they hear, they usually get what they come for .... Our work is, no doubt, greatly affected, for good or evil, by the condition of the congregation ... [21]

To the contrary, it is painfully difficult to preach in settings where a lack of expectation is evident among the congregation. An absence of response predominates: no smile, no tear, no nod of affirmation. The coldness is felt. The white walls seem glacier-like. There is no hunger. There is no longing. There is no expectation. In such settings the word of God will find little, if any, welcome. God's Spirit is quenched in the iciness of the heart. Packer's ominous conclusion is as follows:

> It should be noted ... that while one may effectively put out a fire by dousing it, one cannot make it burn again simply by stopping pouring water; it has to be lighted afresh. Similarly, when the Spirit has been quenched, it is beyond our power to undo the damage we have done; we can only cry to God in penitence, asking that he will revive his work.[22]

As the people of God we must refrain from any kind of attitude or activity that might contribute to a withholding of the effects of the Holy Spirit. As a Person, we must refrain from grieving Him. Christlikeness must prevail within our fellowship so that even our manner of speaking is distinctly Christian. As a Fire, we must refrain from quenching Him. We need to assemble on the Lord's Day having identified ourselves as the people to whom God wants to speak. This is how the congregation contributes to the ministry of the word proclaimed in the power of the Spirit.

> The first symptom of revival which I mention is an unusual thirst for the preaching of the word and unusual meltings of soul under it. Observe how it is with the newborn babe. It thirsts, by the power of an irresistible instinct, after its mother's milk, the destined food and nourishment of its infant life. Just so it is with the heaven-born soul, and with the new-born revived church. It thirsts, by the force of a resistless spiritual instinct, after 'the sincere milk of the word,' the food and nourishment of the immortal soul. In dead souls and dead

churches, there is nothing even approaching to a thirst for the preaching of the word. The people come to the house of God not to satisfy an appetite but to discharge a duty. The most solemn and affecting truths fall powerless on their ears. There are no meltings, no subduings of soul under them. They are scarce listened to without impatience, unless there be something remarkable and exciting in the style and manner of address. Very possibly, eloquence may moisten the eyes and touch the feelings of the people; but the most affecting truths of God fail of reaching their hearts .... The whole of this is reversed in a revived, a living church. The souls of the people there open at once to the word of God, melt and bend beneath the most simple truths presented in the simplest scripture dress. Every opportunity is eagerly embraced. New opportunities are desired and longed for. The word is drunk in with an avidity and delight before unknown .... Let one example suffice from the account of the Isle of Skye: 'It was a common thing, as soon as the Bible was opened, after the preliminary services, and just as the reader began' – here, you will observe, it was the simple reading of the word without preaching – yet such was the power upon the minds of the people that 'it was a common thing for great meltings to come upon the hearers. The deepest attention was paid to every word as the sacred verses were slowly and solemnly enunciated. Then the silent tear might be seen stealing down the rugged but expressive countenances turned upon the reader. It was often a stirring sight to witness the multitudes assembling during the dark winter evenings, to trace their progress as they came in all directions across moors and mountains by the blazing torches which they carried to light their way to the place of meeting. The word of the Lord was precious in those days, and personal inconvenience was little thought of when the hungering soul sought to be satisfied.'[23]

Notes
1. Robert Fleming, *The Fulfilling of the Scripture* (no publisher cited), vol. 1, pp. 365, 378.
2. Charles Haddon Spurgeon, *Lectures to my· Students* (repr. ed., Pasadena: Pilgrim Publications, 1990), p. 154.
3. Jay E. Adams, *A Consumer's Guide to Preaching* (Wheaton: Victor Press, 1991), p. 7.

4. Pierre Ch. Marcel, *The Relevance of Preaching* (Grand Rapids: Baker Book House, 1963), p. 102.

5. Jesus promises a παράκλητος not παράκλησις.

6. G. Abbott Smith, *A Manual Greek Lexicon of the New Testament* (Edinburgh: T & T Clark, 1981), p. 272.

7. Johannes P. Louw and Eugene A. Nida, *Greek-English Lexicon of the New Testament Based on Semantic Domains* (New York: United Bible Societies, 1989), vol. 1, p. 318.

8. 'Just as we should pray for the coming of the Spirit, so we should also pray that the Spirit might not be taken from us. This points to the mysterious truth that although every Christian is indwelt by the Spirit, every Christian is imperfectly united with the Spirit and therefore needs to be possessed more completely by the Spirit.' Donald Bloesch, *Theological Notebook* (Colorado Springs: Helmers and Howard Publishers, 1989), vol. 1, p. 195.

9. John R. W. Stott, *The Message of Ephesians* (Downers Grove: Inter-Varsity Press, 1979), p. 189.

10. Charles Hodge, *A Commentary on the Epistle to the Ephesians* (repr. ed., Grand Rapids: Baker Book House, 1982), p. 275.

11. Charles Haddon Spurgeon, *All-Round Ministry* (repr. ed., Carlisle: The Banner of Truth Trust, 1986), p. 357.

12. Louw and Nida, *A Greek-English Lexicon,* p. 179.

13. R. K. Harrison and Colin Brown, 'σβέννυμι,' *The New International Dictionary of New Testament Theology,* ed. Colin Brown (Grand Rapids: Zondervan Publishing House, 1979), vol. 3, p. 109.

14. Louw and Nida, *A Greek-English Lexicon,* p. 661.

15. William F. Arndt and F. Wilbur Gingrich, *A Greek-English Lexicon of the New Testament and Other Early Christian Literature* (Chicago: The University of Chicago Press, 1979), p. 745.

16. I define prophecy to be the Spirit-given ability to declare the revelation of God, distinct from preaching, the exposition of the previously revealed word.

17. '*To Pneuma* is not to be limited to one specific operation of the Holy Spirit, such as the gift of prophecy (*propheteias,* v. 20). Rather it includes the whole range of gifts discussed by the Apostle in his other writings (1 Cor. 12–14; Eph. 4:11ff.; Rom. 12:3ff.). These gifts were designed for use in the public gatherings of early Christian assemblies, and the writer directs regarding their exercise by means of this brief word.' Robert L. Thomas, *Lexical and Syntactical Exegesis, Synthesis Solutions for 1 Thessalonians* (self-published, 1973), p. 38.

18. Ernest Best, *A Commentary on the First and Second Epistles of the Thessalonians* (New York: Harper & Row Publishers, 1972), p. 238.

19. Thomas, *1 Thessalonians,* p. 38. See also James Everett Frame, *A Critical and Exegetical Commentary on the Epistles of St. Paul to the*

Thessalonians (Edinburgh: T & T Clark, 1953), pp. 203-204 and J. B. Lightfoot, *Notes on the Epistles of St. Paul* (Grand Rapids: William Eerdmans Publishing Company, 1957), pp. 82-83.

20. Eugene Peterson, *The Contemplative Pastor* (Grand Rapids: William B. Eerdmans Publishing Company, 1993), pp. 138-139.

21. Spurgeon, *All-Round,* p. 355.

22. J. I. Packer, *Keep in Step with the Spirit* (Old Tappan: Fleming H. Revell Company, 1984), pp. 252-253.

23. This observation and testimony is attributed to Charles J. Brown without reference in Raymond C. Ortland, Jr., *A Passion for God* (Wheaton: Crossway Books, 1994), pp. 56-57.

10

PRAY ME FULL

Unless I have the power of heaven in the Word of Life I shall die.
WILLIAMS OF PANTYCELYN

It is no marvel that the pulpit is so powerless and ministers so often
disheartened when there are so few to hold up their hands .... O, you
blood bought churches, your ministers need your prayers!
GARDINER SPRING

If you then, being evil, know how to give good gifts
to your children, how much more shall your
heavenly Father give the Holy Spirit to those who ask Him?
JESUS THE CHRIST

Linked With Omnipotence

In 1854 the New Park Street Church extended an invitation to a
young man that he might become their pastor. Their terms were
simple and clear: he would come and preach for a six month
probationary period, at the end of which, an evaluation would
take place and consideration given to a permanent invitation.
The young man, only nineteen years old, countered with a three
month probationary period because, as he said, 'the congregation
might not want me, and I do not wish to be a hindrance.' The
church itself was two hundred years old. It was located in what
was then referred to as the River Flood district of London, an
exceedingly gloomy and repellent section of the city. At the time
of their initial invitation the congregation's membership was
comprised of two hundred and thirty-two people. Only eighty
were present to hear the young candidate's first sermon.

Evidence of God's blessing was directly apparent. Within ten months of his arrival the congregation was forced to move out of their facility to Exeter Hall while the church building was expanded to accommodate the burgeoning crowds. Immediately upon their return, however, the renovations proved inadequate, leaving the congregation with no choice but a return to Exeter Hall. Soon Exeter became too small, with the result that a momentous move was made to the Surrey Gardens Music Hall where, for three years following, this young man preached to as many as ten thousand people each Sunday. In March of 1861 the congregation moved into its new facility, the Metropolitan Tabernacle, where an average of between five and six thousand people gathered weekly. In the first decade of his ministry the church recorded 3,569 baptisms. During the entirety of his pastorate, thirty-eight years, a total of 14,460 people were added to the church.

It was not uncommon for this man to preach ten times a week. It has been estimated that he preached to more than ten million people during his lifetime. On occasion he was known to ask the members of his congregation to remain at home for the following Sunday's service so that newcomers might find a seat. During one service in 1879 the regular congregation was dismissed so that visitors waiting outside might get in. Immediately, the building was filled again. He was the founder of the Stockwell Orphanage, which included four houses for boys and five houses for girls. He began a pastors' college that trained nearly nine hundred men during his lifetime. In 1865 his sermons sold twenty-five thousand copies each week and were translated into more than twenty languages. At least three of his works, including the massive *Metropolitan Tabernacle Pulpit* series, have sold more than one million copies. His book, *All of Grace,* is still the all-time best seller for Moody Press.[1] Undoubtedly, his well-known name has been anticipated: Charles Haddon Spurgeon. Other than Martyn Lloyd-Jones in the present generation, Spurgeon was the last great spokesman for the doctrine to which we have been giving consideration, the vitality of the Spirit.

By his own admission, Spurgeon was a Calvinist. Concerning the salvation of sinners, he made no apology for his confession regarding the sovereignty of God. To Spurgeon, Calvinism was merely a manifestation of faithfulness to the apostolic gospel: 'Puritanism, Protestantism, Calvinism – all poor names which the world has given to our great and glorious faith – the doctrine of Paul the apostle, the gospel of our Lord and Saviour Jesus Christ.'[2] The richness of Spurgeon's Calvinism is especially evident in his resistance to equate divine sovereignty with fatalism. Specific to the concern at hand, Spurgeon steadily refused to disregard the human means that have been divinely appointed to accomplish God's eternal purpose. When, on one occasion, he was asked, 'Mr. Spurgeon, what is your secret?' he replied without hesitation, 'My people pray for me.' Elsewhere he elaborates:

> The sinew of the minister's strength under God is the supplication of his church. We can do anything and everything if we have a praying people around us. But when our dear friends and fellow helpers cease to pray the Holy Ghost hastens to depart, and 'Ichabod' is written on the place of assembly.[3]

> What can we do without your prayers? They link us with the omnipotence of God. Like the lightning rod, they pierce the clouds and bring down the mighty and mysterious power from on high .... The Lord give me a dozen importunate pleaders and lovers of souls, and by his grace we will shake all London from end-to-end.[4]

Only the sovereign Spirit can effect the work of salvation and sanctification. About this Spurgeon would not equivocate. But the decree of God does not undercut human involvement. For this reason, the people of God must learn from Spurgeon's undaunting confidence in the means ordained of God to accomplish His eternal purpose.

In the previous chapter consideration was given to the relationship that exists between the effectual, Spirit-empowered preaching of the word of God and the congregation that assembles to hear the word proclaimed. More particularly, the congregation's first responsibility for preaching was set forth in the following terms: *the congregation must consciously refrain from any kind of attitude or activity that might contribute to a withholding of the effects of the Holy Spirit.* As a person, the Holy Spirit can be grieved by sin, and such grieving can lead to a withdrawal of His influences. Moreover, it is possible for the Spirit and His ministry to be quenched. Thus, it is the responsibility of the congregation to refrain from any kind of attitude or activity that could lead to a removal of His effects. Admittedly, this implied responsibility is remedial in tone. The second congregational responsibility, however, is noticeably more positive and exhortative. It is not concerned with attitudes and actions to be avoided, but with a holy duty to be assumed. In summary, *the congregation must earnestly take up its mandate to make intercession for the effects of the Holy Spirit through the preaching of the word of God.*

Unrelenting Prayer
The Apostle Paul was not a fatalist. Though an avid proponent of God's sovereignty, his simultaneous conviction concerning the indispensability of human instrumentality is steadily exposed. Especially noteworthy is the intercessory emphasis of his ministry. His recorded prayers are among the richest of New Testament texts (*e.g.* Eph. 3:14-21). Moreover, his epistles reveal unashamed requests for prayer on his own behalf. Three of these requests are characterized by a common concern:

> Finally, brethren, pray for us that the word of the Lord may spread rapidly and be glorified, just as it did also with you (2 Thess. 3:1).

> Devote yourselves to prayer, keeping alert in it with an attitude of thanksgiving; praying at the same time for us as well, that God may open up to us a door for the word, so that we may speak forth the mystery of Christ, for which I have also been imprisoned; in order that I may make it clear in the way I ought to speak (Col. 4:2-4).

In both of these passages Paul employs present tense verbs in the imperative mood (*'pray* for us' and *'devote yourselves* to prayer'). Hence, these statements are not delicate suggestions. Nor are they merely reflective of wishful thinking on the part of the Apostle. They are fully authoritative, apostolic commands intended to be carried out continuously, *i.e.* 'Incessantly devote yourselves to prayer on our behalf.' For what purpose are the people of God mandated to pray? '... that the word of the Lord may spread rapidly and be glorified' and 'that God may open up to us a door for the word, so that we may speak forth the mystery of Christ ... that I may make it clear in the way I ought to speak.' No theological ambiguity is to be detected in Paul. God's eternal purpose creates no hesitation where his request for prayer is concerned. Rather, he seeks the ongoing intercession of his readers; in particular, with a view to the effectual proclamation of the evangelical word.

A similar request appears near the conclusion of the Ephesian epistle. In 6:10-20 Paul likens authentic Christianity to a violent battle. Christians will wage war, not only against the sinful inclinations of their own residual depravity and the rebellious world system, but 'against the spiritual forces of wickedness in the heavenly places' (Eph. 6:12). But the Christian need not cower in fear. God Himself has supplied adequate resources in Jesus Christ. To illustrate these resources, Paul draws upon imagery easily identifiable to his readers: a Roman soldier dressed in full battle array.

After identifying each piece of armor (6:14-17), Paul then turns his attention toward the subject of prayer (6:18-20). He does so, but not because prayer is a component part of the battle array. Appropriate analogy has already been made to each of the six pieces of armor commonly worn by Roman soldiers (belt, breastplate, shoes, shield, helmet, sword). Paul concludes the armor metaphor in verse 17. From that point he seeks to establish the principle source of strength in which the warfare is to be successfully fought. Hodge adds wise perspective:

It is not armor or weapons which make the warrior. There must be courage and strength; and even then he often needs help. As the Christian has no resources of strength in himself, and can succeed only as aided from above, the apostle urges the duty of prayer.[5]

The source of strength for the battle is external to the Christian. It is to be found in God through the means He has appointed. Hence, Paul petitions his readers:

With all prayer and petition pray at all times in the Spirit, and with this in view, be on the alert with all perseverance and petition for all the saints, and pray on my behalf (Eph. 6:18-19a).

Such a request from Paul is expected. But for what specific purpose does Paul exhort the Ephesians to make intercession?

... that utterance may be given to me in the opening of my mouth, to make known with boldness the mystery of the gospel, for which I am an ambassador in chains; that in proclaiming it I may speak boldly, as I ought to speak (Eph. 6:19b-20).

Considerable attention could be given to these verses. For the present concern it is sufficient only to note the primary emphasis governing Paul's request for prayer, an emphasis that is expressed objectively and subjectively.[6] Speaking objectively, Paul seeks 'that utterance may be given'. The noun $\lambda \acute{o} \gamma o s$ is used 'with primary focus upon the content of communication — word, saying, message, statement ...'[7] It is especially important to note that Paul considers this utterance to be a gift.[8] But what is this 'utterance' to which Paul refers? He supplies a subjective description: 'to make known with boldness the mystery of the gospel ... that in proclaiming it I may speak boldly ...' Stated simply, this 'utterance' sought by Paul is a gift from God to speak the gospel with an identifiable boldness. Though earlier consideration was given to the definition of the term ($\pi\alpha\rho\rho\eta\sigma\acute{\iota}\alpha$, chap. 7), the emphasis here is to suggest that its manifestation originates from a supernatural source. Properly speaking, this boldness in preaching the gospel is a gift from God.

It is interesting to observe that what is here described as a gift from God is elsewhere attributed to the filling with the Holy Spirit. In Acts 4:13, as a consequence of being filled with the Spirit, Peter's preaching is identified in these same terms: 'Now as they observed the confidence (παρρησία) of Peter ...' In the same chapter the Christians pray for this boldness in proclamation: '... grant that Thy bond-servants may speak Thy word with all confidence' (παρρησία) (Acts 4:29). Two verses later Luke records the answer to their request: '... and they were all filled with the Holy Spirit, and began to speak the word of God with boldness' (παρρησία) (Acts 4:31). This boldness in speaking the word of God, so zealously sought by Paul as a divine gift, is a consequence of the Spirit's work. It is for this reason Paul besought the Ephesians to pray on his behalf. His understanding of the sovereign Spirit did in no way impede his commitment to the God-appointed means; and here, in particular, as it relates to the responsibility given to the people of God. 'Pray for the effects of the Spirit as I preach.'

The Spirit of the Church
The congregation has been given certain responsibilities for the preaching of the word of God. As has been seen, the New Testament mandates the people of God to make intercession for the effects of the Holy Spirit through the preaching of the scriptures. To be sure, this has direct bearing on Christians as individuals. Each Christian needs to recognize his appointed duty to make consistent supplication for the Spirit's blessing on behalf of himself, the preacher, and others who will come under the sound of the proclaimed word. During the Great Awakening it was the practice of a Welsh pastor to teach the following prayer to new converts: 'Unless I have the power of heaven in the Word of Life I shall die.'[9]

This congregational responsibility also has implications for Christian families. The most effective manner for instructing children in this doctrine of the Spirit's vitality is for parents to consistently pray with their children for this blessing to attend the preaching of the word. On several occasions my own children have asked: 'Daddy, why do you always pray for the Holy Spirit to help you when you preach?' To which I have replied, 'Because we want God's word to be accompanied by power. This is how God changes people. By God's grace you will come to experience this yourselves.'

Most importantly, this intercessory responsibility has direct bearing on Christians as an assembled people. Aware of their absolute dependence upon divine enablement, congregations need regularly to make petition for the transforming effects of the Spirit through the preaching of the word. This can occur during the worship service, in Bible studies, discipleship groups, and Christian education classes. Moreover, local congregations need to give serious consideration to prayer meetings that are altogether devoted to this concern. Marcel is particularly pointed here:

If a believer ... is inclined to conclude that his pastor does not preach, let him know that he, a believer, and the Church with him bear more responsibility for it than the pastor himself. We have not spoken of the Spirit whom the preacher alone is to receive, but of the Spirit of the Church, whom the Church, i.e., each believer, entreats and from whom he simply receives his share. The lot of a people of God is to hear the preaching of the word, which people he wishes to bless by hearing and answering their prayers .... Does such a people exist in each of our churches? Who would dare presume as much? How is the worship hour prepared for and celebrated? In what atmosphere? It is especially disturbing how few believers pray seriously for these things and how great a number overlook this indispensable element. Even in the sanctuary, relatively few invoke the Spirit with perseverance and with definite aims in mind. Some apparently think triflingly of it, since they arrive late. Practically nowhere are there meetings of prayer before the worship hour. Such negligence tends to dispel the Spirit and contributes to rendering the preaching ineffective for a number of hearers, simultaneously depriving the preacher of his most substantial support. When, then, will the believers en masse understand that they are primarily responsible for the preaching which they hear, yes, more than their preachers? If every pastor knew and felt that the congregation was praying and that each member had prayed, that the congregation was supporting him, interceding for him, that each member had benevolent feelings for the man whom God had given to instruct in salvation, that each one loved him in God, what preacher would not feel himself a new man? and whose preaching would not be transformed. Once again, preaching the word is a function and activity of the Church, not the function and specialty of a man. Before judging anyone, the believers should know that if they do not prepare for the preaching as we have just indicated they will receive very little, perhaps nothing.[10]

Gardiner Spring addresses the same concern:

It is a delightful thought to a young man entering upon the ministry of reconciliation that, unworthy as he is, the prayers of thousands of God's people are continually going up, on his behalf, to his Father and their Father, to his God and their God. He seems to hear the church of God saying to him, We cannot go to this sacred work, but we will follow you with our prayers! He seems to hear many a Christian parent say to him, We have no son to send to this hallowed vocation; but go *you* to it, and you shall not lack an interest in our prayers! .... how full of encouragement to the heart that trembles under a view of the responsibilities of the sacred office! how delightful this spiritual impetus to a mind almost ready to sink under its own conscious infirmities! And how unspeakably precious the thought to all who labour in this great work, whether in youthful, or riper years, that they are thus habitually remembered in the prayers of the churches! Let the thought sink deep into the heart of every church, that their minister will be very much such a minister as their prayers may make him. If nothing short of Omnipotent grace can make a Christian, nothing less than this can make a faithful and successful minister of the gospel.[11]

Dutch pastors often recite a familiar saying to their congregations. Though it defies exact translation into English, it can be summarized as follows: 'If you pray me full, I'll preach you full.'[12] Do evangelical congregations 'pray their pastors full?' Most, it must be acknowledged, do not. Yet this is their mandate. This is their holy responsibility. Pursuing this is a sure indication of the Spirit's preliminary work.[13] Apart from it, however, very little progress can be anticipated. The people of God need to take up their responsibility to make intercession for the effects of the Holy Spirit through the preaching of the word of God.

Confident In The Promise

One of the distinct features of the Gospel of Luke is the frequent mention of Jesus Christ in the act of prayer. The third Gospel records more citations of Jesus praying than do the Gospels of Matthew, Mark, and John combined. On one of these well-known occasions Jesus is approached by an unnamed disciple with a specific petition: 'Lord, teach us to pray just as John also taught his disciples' (Luke 11:1). Graciously, Jesus answers his request and supplies His followers with a pattern to emulate (Luke 11:2-4). At the conclusion of this prayer, Jesus then takes the opportunity to develop two related concerns: (1) the need of the believer to persevere in prayer (11:5-11); and, (2) the eagerness of the Father to respond to His asking children (11:11-13). Regarding this second concern Jesus states:

> Now suppose one of you fathers is asked by his son for a fish; he will not give him a snake instead of a fish, will he? Or if he is asked for an egg, he will not give him a scorpion, will he? (Luke 11:11-12).

A good man would never give an evil gift to his child. To do so would be contrary to his nature. What is perplexing, however, is that an evil man would give a good gift to his child. Such an act is in radical contradiction with his nature. Yet this contradiction is expressed on a daily basis because, though polluted by depravity, every father loves his child and would spare no expense to do him good. Jesus sets forth this self-evident principle, but then moves ahead to argue from the lesser to the greater:

> If you then, being evil, know how to give good gifts to your children, how much more shall your heavenly Father give the Holy Spirit to those who ask Him? (Luke 11:13).

God is eager to give the Holy Spirit to His asking children. 'But,' it may be asked, 'to what specifically is Jesus here referring?' The answer is found in the slight variation that exists in the Matthean account of these words:

> If you then, being evil, know how to give good gifts to your children, how much more shall your Father who is in heaven give what is good to those who ask Him! (Matt. 7:11).

Matthew's version asserts that the Father is eager to give 'what is good' to His asking children. Luke's account acknowledges the readiness of the Father to give 'the Holy Spirit' to His asking children. Are these two accounts contradictory? No, they are mutually explanatory. As has been stated earlier, the Holy Spirit is the source of all that is good and beneficial in the life of the Christian. Jesus, therefore, wants to assure His disciples that their heavenly Father is eager to dispense the good gifts that come from the sovereign Spirit; that is, the supernatural effects of which He alone is the direct cause.

> One should think it impossible to ... doubt whether special Divine influence be necessary for the conversion of the soul, or whether the communication of it be a prerogative of Divine sovereignty .... Still there is every ground to expect the influence we need. It is our privilege to live under the dispensation of the Spirit, as well as under that of the Messiah. The former of these is connected with the latter: or perhaps more correctly speaking they are identical; the covenant established in Christ's blood is the economy of the Spirit. The ministry of reconciliation is the ministry of the Spirit. I do not mean to represent this divine influence as confined to the Christian economy, for since the beginning of time no soul has been converted or sanctified but by this heavenly power; but the communications of it before the coming of Christ were limited, partial, and scanty, compared with what they have been since: they constituted not the shower, but only the drops which precede it. Hence the language of the evangelist, 'This spake He of the Spirit, which they that believe on him should receive, for the Holy Ghost was not yet given, because that Jesus was not yet glorified.' This idea, that we are under the

Spirit's economy, should enlarge our expectations of rich communications of this invaluable and essential blessing. The view I have given of Divine sovereignty is not intended, nor when rightly understood, is it calculated, to discourage hope, but simply to teach dependence. While God reserves to himself the right of bestowment, and acts upon his own rules of communication, he warrants and invites the most comprehensive requests, and the largest anticipations. Since he has promised to give the boon in answer to the prayer of faith, it would seem to be our own fault that we have it not in more abounding measure. The very recollection of our privilege in being placed under such an economy, might seem to be enough to call forth our prayers and to awaken our expectations. Instead of being surprised that so much of this Divine power accompanies our ministries in the most successful periods of our history, we should be surprised that we receive so little of it, and enquire after the obstructing cause. In a country like Egypt, where rain seldom falls, a shower is the exception, and a dry atmosphere the general rule; but in our variable climate, a long drought is the rarity, and the frequent shower is the common occurrence. The husbandman ploughs and sows in this land, with the expectant eyes upon the heavens, and feels disappointed if the fertilizing rain is withheld. So it should be with us, in reference to the shower of God's grace. We are not in the dry and arid atmosphere of the Levitical economy, but enjoy the privilege of the dew-distilling, rain-dropping dispensation of the Spirit; and with us the question should be, why we have not more of this Divine influence, and what has provoked the Lord to withhold from us the genial influences of his grace. Instead of being at any time astonished that our ministry is so much blessed, we should enquire why it is not always so. When we consider what is said, that God 'willed not the death of a sinner, but would rather that he should repent, and turn from his wickedness and live;' when we recollect what he has done for the salvation of sinners; when we add to this, that the gospel is his own truth, and preaching his own institution, we are sometimes ready to wonder that he does not pour out that influence which is necessary to give effect to the purposes of his own benevolence, and almost to inquire, 'What does the Lord now wait for?' In answer to this it may be replied, 'He waits for the earnest labours of his ministers, the faith of his church, and the believing prayers of both.'[14]

As I write these words I am filled with great expectation. I read of nothing in the scriptures which would indicate that the vitality of the Spirit was a temporary phenomena, an exclusive manifestation of power for an epoch long ago. Quite to the contrary, it has been my reading of history, particularly the periods of the Reformation and the First and Second Great Awakenings, that has filled me with a holy covetousness for this blessing of the Spirit of God in preaching.

We have been ordained to a time of significant influence. Many of us find ourselves in churches surrounded by hundreds of thousands of people who have no idea that God Himself has sent a Redeemer for sinners. It is a great moment to know the gospel. It is a great moment to be a preacher. It is a great moment to possess the promise: the eagerness of our Father to bless His asking children with the good gifts that come from the Spirit of the living God.

Will you ask for the Spirit's power to accompany the preaching of the evangelical word? Let us not give rest to our heavenly Father until He hears our collective cries for the vitality of the Spirit. On this basis alone will Christ's kingdom advance.

Notes
1. Eric W. Hayden, 'Did You Know? A Collection of True and Unusual Facts About Charles Haddon Spurgeon,' *Christians History* (Volume X, No. 1), pp. 2-3.
2. Charles Haddon Spurgeon, *An All-Round Ministry* (repr. ed., Carlisle: The Banner of Truth Trust, 1986), p. 160.
3. _____, *The Metropolitan Tabernacle Pulpit* (repr. ed., Pasadena: Pilgrim Publications, 1980), vol. 25, p. 695.
4. *Ibid.*, vol. 23, p. 445.
5. Charles Hodge, *A Commentary on the Epistle to the Ephesians* (repr. ed., Grand Rapids: Baker Book House, 1980), pp. 389-390.
6. T. K. Abbott, *A Critical and Exegetical Commentary on the Epistles to the Ephesians and to the Colossians* (Edinburgh: T & T Clark, 1979), p. 189.
7. Johannes P. Louw and Eugene A. Nida, *Greek-English Lexicon of the New Testament Based on Semantic Domains* (New York: United Bible Societies, 1989), vol. 1, p. 400.
8. δοθῇ has the position of emphasis.

9. This prayer is attributed without reference to Williams of Pantycelyn in Eifion Evans, *Daniel Rowland and the Great Evangelical Awakening in Wales* (Carlisle: The Banner of Truth Trust, 1985), p. 367.

10. Pierre Ch. Marcel, *The Relevance of Preaching* (Grand Rapids: Baker Book House, 1963), pp. 101-102.

11. Gardiner Spring, *The Power of the Pulpit* (repr. ed., Carlisle: The Banner of Truth Trust, 1986), pp. 222-223.

12. This quotation was given by Dr. Joel Beeke in a class at Westminster Seminary entitled 'Experimental Preaching'.

13. 'As with the truth that is preached, prayer has no inherent power in itself. On the contrary, true prayer is bound up with a persuasion of our inability and our complete dependence on God. Prayer, considered as a human activity, whether offered by few or by many, can guarantee no results. But prayer that throws believers in heartfelt need on God, with true concern for the salvation of sinners, will not go unanswered. Prayer of this kind precedes blessing, not because of any necessary cause and effect, but because such prayer secures an acknowledgement of the true Author of the blessing. And where such a spirit of prayer exists it is a sign that God is already intervening to advance his cause.' Iain H. Murray, *Revival and Revivalism: The Making and Marring of American Evangelicalism* (Carlisle: The Banner of Truth Trust, 1994), p. 129.

14. John Angell James, *An Earnest Ministry* (repr. ed., Carlisle: The Banner of Truth Trust, 1993), pp. 286-289.

SUMMARY

With preaching Christianity stands or falls.
P.T. FORSYTH

Pastors are sinners ... they know fear and trembling
whenever they mount the pulpit. They are crushed by the
feeling of being poor human beings who are probably more
unworthy than all those who sit before them.
KARL BARTH

God is the preacher.
MARTIN LUTHER

Following a presentation of this material to some of the faculty
members at Westminster Seminary in California, one of the
professors posed a question to which I had given no prior
consideration. 'Mr Azurdia,' he asked, 'have you personally
experienced this "vitality of the Spirit" in your own preaching?'
Ready in my arsenal of answers were responses to anticipated
questions concerning issues of exegesis and theology. This
question, however, clearly of a more personal and experiential
nature, had been altogether unanticipated. Though the professor
had no malicious intention in view, I felt exposed as the seconds
of silent response to his question seemed like hours.

In desperation I thought to myself, 'If I answer "Yes, I have
experienced this ministry of the Spirit in my preaching," I run the
risk of appearing exceedingly arrogant. Who am I to declare this
blessing for myself?' But then (in what I am sure was a moment
of carnal self-preservation!) the implication of an answer to the
contrary became equally apparent. 'If I answer "No" in a kind of
sanctimonious piety, then what kind of credibility can be given
to my conclusions?' It was an awkward moment, to say the least.
Nevertheless, it was a pertinent and necessary question.

There have been those occasional moments in preaching when I have become mindful of an other-worldly kind of enablement; when my thoughts concerning the Scriptures were suddenly made free from all apparent impediments, when my affections for Jesus Christ and the well-being of souls were unusually intensified, when words and phrases came with ease and precision. More commonly, however, my experience in preaching has not been so dramatic. To be sure, never once have I felt anything less than a thorough-going confidence in the integrity and authority of the biblical text. Nor have I ever felt that the act of preaching itself was perfunctory. But to suggest that I am thoroughly conscious of the effects of my preaching at the conclusion of each Lord's Day would be less than honest. Though I preach to a wonderfully responsive congregation, frequently I have no immediate and personal sense of the effectiveness of my preaching.

All of this to now say that it has not been my intention to posit myself as the exemplar of all for which I have contended in these pages. My purpose has been an attempt to establish a biblical theology of Spirit empowered preaching and, in so doing, to stimulate others toward more careful and critical thought in this vitally essential, albeit mysterious, field of study. I would summarize my conclusions in the following three statements:

1) *Spirit empowered preaching is the principle means of advancing the kingdom of Jesus Christ.* We must never lose sight of the fact that Jesus gave Himself to the ministry of proclamation (Matt. 4:17; Mark 1:38), this being the stated reason for which He was empowered by the Holy Spirit (Luke 4:18-19). Moreover, it should be noted that He commissioned His disciples to this same task. Hence, they, too, would be clothed with the power of the Spirit (Luke 24:49). Finally, it is evident that this same methodology for advancing the gospel was passed on to subsequent Christian leaders (2 Tim. 4:2). It is essential that evangelicals come to understand that methodology is not neutral when the gospel is in view. Although small group Bible studies, Sunday School classes, Christian literature, and musical

concerts may be useful, the church of Jesus Christ has been given an authoritative message to declare. 'Preaching God's word is the central gift of the Spirit given by Christ to the church.'[1]

2) *Spirit empowered preaching will be evangelical in emphasis.* The central theme of the Bible is God's redemptive program in Jesus Christ. Until this fact begins to shape our interpretive approach to the Scriptures Christian preaching will lack the accompanying power of the Spirit of God, whose stated purpose it is to glorify Jesus Christ in and through the Scriptures. To be sure, the most basic part of understanding a biblical text begins with grammatical-historical exegesis. But to conclude that this meaning is the entire and exclusive meaning of the text is more a reflection of post-Enlightenment rationalism than of the Bible's use of itself.

Over and again the biblical writers use the Old Testament in ways that often unsettle evangelicals. To curb their anxieties, they often retort, 'Well, the apostles may treat the text as such because they are inspired. But we have no warrant to do so.' To the contrary, the Bible's use of itself 'provides the richest path we have toward understanding the Bible's self-hermeneutic and gives us the material for establishing a genuinely biblical basis for our own hermeneutic'.[2] Jesus Himself stresses that the entirety of the Old Testament Scriptures serve as a signpost to Him (Luke 24:25-27, 44-47). Moreover, the literary structure of entire New Testament epistles reveal that moral imperatives grow out of redemptive indicatives.

This singleness of hermeneutic goal, with its focus on Christ, means that the Bible is primarily a book about God and humankind's relationship to him. Specific life problems are therefore only secondarily addressed. If we lose sight of the primary hermeneutical goal in order to seek for specific answers to our specific problems, we miss the mark, for very few of the 'difficult' modern situational problems are directly addressed in the Bible. The Bible instills in us the knowledge of God. If we do know him, then our character is transformed, and we can confront the exigent contemporary problems as the people of God, not as people armed with a comprehensive book of casuistic answers.[3]

To seek the Spirit's power in preaching necessitates a harmonious correspondence to the purpose of His Word.

3) *Spirit-empowered preaching is the responsibility of the Church.* Does the Church long to hear more than religious platitudes and moralisms when she assembles on the Lord's Day? Does the Church seek more from her pulpits than recitations of biblical history and displays of theological acumen? Does the Church hunger for a heaven-dispatched word concerning Jesus Christ and her relationship to Him? If the answer to these questions are in the affirmative, then it is time for the Church to recognize and assume her responsibility for this ministry of proclamation.

To be sure, she must allow, and even insist, that her ministers be devoted to this task. They are to be men who study diligently, pray fervently, and stay poignantly mindful of their inherent weaknesses. But the Church herself must also take up her role in this ministry. Anything that grieves the Holy Spirit, especially sins of the tongue, must not be tolerated in her fellowship. She must bring to the act of preaching a longing to hear the voice of God, an enthusiastic readiness to hear and obey. Finally, she must give a fresh hearing to the apostolic petitions:

'... pray for us that the word of the Lord may spread rapidly and be glorified ...' (2 Thess. 3:1)

'Devote yourselves to prayer ... so that we may speak forth the mystery of Christ ...' (Col. 4:2-4)

'With all prayer and petition pray at all times in the Spirit ... that utterance may be given to me in the opening of my mouth to make known with boldness the mystery of the gospel ... that in proclaiming it I may speak boldly, as I ought to speak' (Eph. 6:18-20).

When the Church gathers to hear messages of political activism and pop psychology, prayer is infrequent and token. But when the Church longs for men to bring into her pulpits the very atmosphere of heaven itself, she turns her attention toward intercession. She will pray for her ministers: that God might open their eyes to see the beauties of Jesus Christ on the pages of sacred Scripture, that God might give clarity and boldness of speaking when these men ascend into her pulpits on the Lord's Day.

She will pray for the hearers of the Word: that God might sanctify believers and powerfully transform sinners. When the Church languishes for the word of life she will find ways to beseech the throne of grace.

> We have a concert of prayer for the heathen, another for Sabbath schools, and another for the blessing of God upon the distribution of religious tracts. Why should we overlook the great means of God's own appointment for the salvation of men? May there not be something in the form of a concert of prayer for the ministers of the Gospel? If nothing better can be suggested, why may there not be a general understanding among Christian men, and Christian families, to set apart the morning of every Lord's Day, for this great and special object?... The time is a fitting one; and such a service would not fail to exert a delightful influence on the privileges of the sanctuary. 'Before they call I will answer; and while they are yet speaking I will hear.' Should God give to the churches the spirit of prayer for their ministers, it would be with the purpose of answering it.... If you ever enter into the 'secret place' of the Most High, and get near the heart of him your souls love, plead earnestly that his own power may attend the stated ministrations of his Gospel. If you ever lie on Jesus' bosom, remember us. Open your desires; tell your Immanuel of his costly sacrifice and his wonderful love; tell him of his power and our weakness; speak to him of unutterable glory, and the interminable anguish beyond the grave. With tears of solicitude urge your suit, and tell him that he has committed the treasure of earthen vessels, that the excellency of the power may be all of God.[4]

Notes

1. Sinclair B. Ferguson, *The Holy Spirit* (Downers Grove: InterVarsity Press, 1996), p. 239.

2. Dan G. McCartney, 'The New Testament's Use of the Old Testament', *Inerrancy and Hermeneutic*, ed. Harvie M. Conn (Grand Rapids: Baker Book House, 1988), p.102.

3. *Ibid.*, p.114.

4. Gardiner Spring, *The Power of the Pulpit* (repr. ed., Carlisle: The Banner of Truth Trust, 1986), pp. 226-227.

BIBLIOGRAPHY

Monographs

Adams, Jay E., *A Consumer's Guide to Preaching*. Wheaton: Victor Press, 1991.

_____, *How to Help People Change*. Grand Rapids: Zondervan Publishing House, 1986.

_____, *Preaching with Purpose*. Grand Rapids: Zondervan Publishing House, 1982.

_____, *Truth Applied*. Grand Rapids: Zondervan Publishing House, 1990.

Alexander, J. W., *Thoughts on Preaching*. Carlisle: The Banner of Truth Trust, 1988 (repr. ed.).

Barth, Karl, *Homiletics*. Louisville: Westminster/John Knox Press, 1991 (trans. by Geoffrey W. Bromiley and Donald E. Daniels).

Baumann, J. Daniel, *An Introduction to Contemporary Preaching*. Grand Rapids: Baker Book House, 1972.

Bloesch, Donald, *Essentials of Evangelical Theology*. San Francisco: HarperCollins Publishers, 1978.

_____, *God The Almighty*. Downers Grove: InterVarsity Press, 1995.

_____, *Theological Notebook*. Colorado Springs: Helmers & Howard, Publishers, 1989.

Bounds, E. M., *Power Through Prayer*. Grand Rapids: Baker Book House, 1972 (repr. ed.).

Bridges, Charles, *The Christian Ministry*. Carlisle: The Banner of Truth Trust, 1991 (repr. ed.).

Burgess, Stanley M., *The Holy Spirit: Ancient Christian Traditions*. Peabody: Hendrickson Publishers, Inc., 1984.

_____, *The Holy Spirit: Medieval Roman Catholic and Reformation Traditions*. Peabody: Hendrickson Publishers, Inc., 1997.

Calvin, John, *Institutes of the Christian Religion*. Philadelphia: The Westminster Press, 1960 (repr. ed., 2 vols.) (trans. by Ford Lewis Battles).

Chapell, Brian, *Christ-Centered Preaching*. Grand Rapids: Baker Books, 1994.

Dallimore, Arnold, *George Whitefield: The Life and Times of the Great Evangelist of the 18th Century Revival*. Carlisle: The Banner of Trust Trust, 1970 (2 vols.).

Eby, David, *Power Preaching*. Ross-Shire: Christian Focus Publications, 1996.

Evans, Eifion, *Daniel Rowland and the Great Evangelical Awakening in Wales*. Carlisle: The Banner of Truth Trust, 1985.

Fee, Gordon D., *God's Empowering Presence*. Peabody: Hendrickson Publishers, Inc., 1994.

Fish, Henry C., *Power in the Pulpit*. Carlisle: The Banner of Truth Trust, n.d.

Green, Michael, *I Believe in the Holy Spirit*. William B. Eerdmans Publishing Company, 1975.

Greidanus, Sidney, *The Modern Preacher and the Ancient Text*. Grand Rapids: William B. Eerdmans Publishing Company, 1988.

Henry, Carl F. H., ed., *Revelation and the Bible*. Grand Rapids: Baker Book House, 1958.

Hildebrandt, Wilf, *An Old Testament Theology of the Spirit of God*. Peabody: Hendrickson Publishers, Inc., 1995.

James, John Angell, *An Earnest Ministry*. Carlisle: The Banner of Truth Trust, 1993 (repr. ed.).

Kelly, Douglas, *Preachers with Power: Four Stalwarts of the South*. Carlisle: The Banner of Truth Trust, 1992.

Lewis, Peter, *The Genius of Puritanism*. Haywards Heath Sussex: Carey Publications, 1979.

Lloyd-Jones, D. Martyn, *Authority*. Carlisle: The Banner of Truth Trust, 1992 (repr. ed.).

_____, *Joy Unspeakable*. Wheaton: Harold Shaw Publishers, 1984.

_____, *Preaching & Preachers*. Grand Rapids: Zondervan Publishing House, 1971.

_____, *The Puritans: Their Origins and Successors*. Carlisle: The Banner of Truth Trust, 1987.

Logan, Samuel, ed., *The Preacher and Preaching*. Phillipsburg: Presbyterian and Reformed Publishing Company, 1986.

Marcel, Pierre C., *The Relevance of Preaching*. Grand Rapids: Baker Book House, 1963.

McKim, Donald K., ed., *Readings in Calvin's Theology*. Grand Rapids: Baker Book House, 1984.

Miller, Calvin, *Spirit, Word, and Story*. Dallas: Word Publishing, 1989.

Morris, Leon, *Spirit of the Living God*. London: Inter-Varsity Press, 1974.

Murray, Iain H., *D. Martyn Lloyd-Jones*. Carlisle: The Banner of Truth Trust, 1990 (2 vols.).

_____, *The Puritan Hope*. Carlisle: The Banner of Truth Trust, 1971.

_____, *Revival and Revivalism*. Carlisle: The Banner of Truth Trust, 1994.

Nuttall, Geoffrey F., *The Holy Spirit in Puritan Faith and Experience*. Chicago: The University of Chicago Press, 1992.

Owen, John, 'The Holy Spirit' (*The Works of John Owen,* vol. 3). Carlisle: The Banner of Truth Trust, 1979 (repr. ed., 16 vols.).

_____, 'The Work of the Spirit' (*The Works of John Owen,* vol. 4). Carlisle: The Banner of Truth Trust, 1979 (repr. ed., 16 vols.).

Packer, J. I., *Keep in Step with the Spirit*. Old Tappan: Fleming H. Revell Company, 1984.

_____, *A Quest for Godliness*. Wheaton: Crossway Books, 1990.

_____, *Truth and Power*. Wheaton: Harold Shaw Publishers, 1996.

Perkins, William, *The Art of Prophesying*. Carlisle: The Banner of Trust Trust, 1996 (repr. ed.).

Piper, John, *The Supremacy of God in Preaching*. Grand Rapids: Baker Book House, 1990.

Ramm, Bernard, *After Fundamentalism*. San Francisco: Harper & Row, Publishers, 1983.

Ryken, Leland, *Worldly Saints*. Grand Rapids: Zondervan Publishing House, 1986.

Sargent, Tony, *The Sacred Anointing*. Wheaton: Crossway Books, 1994.

Spring, Gardiner, *The Power of the Pulpit*. Carlisle: The Banner of Truth Trust, 1986 (repr. ed.).

Spurgeon, Charles, *An All-Round Ministry*. Carlisle: The Banner of Truth Trust, 1986 (repr. ed.).

_____, *Lectures to my Students*. Pasadena: Pilgrim Publications, 1990 (repr. ed.).

Stott, John R. W., *The Baptism and Fullness of the Holy Spirit*. Downers Grove: Inter-Varsity Press, 1964.

_____, *Between Two Worlds: The Art of Preaching in the Twentieth Century*. Grand Rapids: William B. Eerdmans Publishing Company, 1982.

_____, *The Preacher's Portrait*. Grand Rapids: William B. Eerdmans Publishing Company, 1961.

Vinet, A., *Homiletics*. New York: Ivison And Phinney Publishers, 1854 (trans. and ed. by Thomas H. Skinner).

Winslow, Octavius, *The Work of the Holy Spirit*. Carlisle: The Banner of Truth Trust, 1991 (repr. ed.).

Zuck, Roy B., *Teaching with Spiritual Power*. Grand Rapids: Kregel Publications, 1993.

Commentaries

Abbott, T. K., *A Critical and Exegetical Commentary on the Epistles to the Ephesians and to the Colossians*. Edinburgh: T & T Clark, 1979.

Barrrett, C. K., *The First Epistle to the Corinthians*. Peabody: Hendrickson Publishers, 1968.

Beasley-Murray, George R., *John*. Waco: Word Books, Publisher, 1987.

Bernard, J. H., *A Critical and Exegetical Commentary on the Gospel According to St. John*. Edinburgh: T & T Clark, 1985 (repr. ed., 2 vols.).

Calvin, John, *The First Epistle of Paul to the Corinthians*. Grand Rapids: William B. Eerdmans Publishing Company, 1973 (repr. ed.).

_____, *Galatians, Ephesians, Philippians and Colossians*. Grand Rapids: William B. Eerdmans Publishing Company, 1965 (repr. ed.).

_____, *The Gospel According To St. John*. Grand Rapids: William B. Eerdmans Publishing Company, 1974 (repr. ed., 2 vols.).

Carson, D. A., *The Cross and the Christian Ministry: An Exposition of Passages from 1 Corinthians*. Grand Rapids: Baker Book House, 1993.

_____, *The Farewell Discourse and Final Prayer of Jesus*. Grand Rapids: Baker Book House, 1980.

_____, *The Gospel According to John*. Grand Rapids: William B. Eerdmans Publishing Company, 1991.

Conzelmann, Hans, *A Commentary on the First Epistle to the Corinthians*. Philadelphia: Fortress Press, 1975.

Dods, Marcus, *The Gospel of St. John*. Grand Rapids: William B. Eerdmans Publishing Company, 1980.

Ellingworth, Paul and Hatton, Howard A., *Paul's First Letter to the Corinthians*. New York: United Bible Societies, 1994.

Fee, Gordon D., *The First Epistle to the Corinthians*. Grand Rapids: William B. Eerdmans Publishing Company, 1987.

Findlay, G. G., *St. Paul's First Epistle to the Corinthians*. Grand Rapids: William B. Eerdmans Publishing Company, 1980.

Grosheide, F. W., *Commentary on the First Epistle to the Corinthians*. Grand Rapids: William B. Eerdmans Publishing Company, 1953.

Hendrikson, William, *Exposition of the Gospel According to John*. Grand Rapids: Baker Book House, 1953.

_____, *Galatians and Ephesians*. Grand Rapids: Baker Book House, 1979.

_____, *Thessalonians, Timothy and Titus*. Grand Rapids: Baker Book House, 1979.

Hodge, Charles, *A Commentary on the Epistle to the Ephesians*. Grand Rapids: Baker Book House, 1982 (repr. ed.).

_____, *1 & 2 Corinthians*. Carlisle: The Banner of Truth Trust, 1994 (repr.).

Kistemaker, Simon J., *1 Corinthians*. Grand Rapids: Baker Book House, 1993.

Lloyd-Jones, D. Martyn., *The Christian Soldier: An Exposition of Ephesians 6:10-20*. Grand Rapids: Baker Book House, 1977.

_____, *Darkness and Light: An Exposition of Ephesians 4:17—5:17*. Grand Rapids: Baker Book House, 1982.

Moffatt, James, *The First and Second Epistle to the Thessalonians*. William B. Eerdmans Publishing Company, 1980.

Morris, Leon, *The Gospel According to John*. Grand Rapids: William B. Eerdmans Publishing Company, 1971.

Newman, Barclay M., and Nida, Eugene, *A Translators Handbook on the Gospel of John*. New York: United Bible Societies, 1980.

Robertson, Archibald and Plummer, Alfred, *A Critical and Exegetical Commentary on the First Epistle of St. Paul to the Corinthians*. Edinburgh: T & T Clark, 1994.

Ryle, J. C., *Expository Thoughts on the Gospels*. Grand Rapids: Baker Book House, 1990 (repr. ed., 4 vols.).

Salmond, S. D. F., *The Epistle to the Ephesians*. Grand Rapids: William B. Eerdmans Publishing Company, 1980.

Stott, John R. W., *The Message of Ephesians*. Downers Grove: Inter-Varsity Press, 1979.

Thomas, Robert L., *Lexical and Syntactical Exegesis, Synthesis, Solutions*. Self-Published, 1973.

SCRIPTURE INDEX

Genesis
8:21 41

Numbers
11:29 104
24:2ff 104

Deuteronomy
33:1 147

2 Samuel
23:2 104

2 Chronicles
8:14 147
24:20 104

Nehemiah
9:30 104

Psalms
51:11 155
119:18 47
139:7 134

Ecclesiastes
9:3 41

Isaiah
53:1 117
63:10 154

Jeremiah
17:9 13

Ezekiel
11:5 104
36:27 24

Matthew
3:11 157
4:17 84
4:23 78
6:9 153
6:31-33 153
7:11 174
9:35 78
10: 7 20
10:29-30 153
11:1 78
11:27 43
12:31-32 154
14:25-31 21
21:44 130
28:19 154

Mark
1:38 84
3:14 20, 84
9:33-37 21
16:15 74, 85

Luke
1:13-15 105
1:16-17 105
1:42-45 106
1:39-41 106
1:67-79 106
2:34 130
3:16 157
3:21-22 118
4:1 114, 118
4:14 118
4:15 78
4:18-19 84, 119
4:21 59
4:44 78
5:1-10 122
9:52-55 21
11:1 173

11:2-4 173
11:5-11 173
11:11-12 173
11:13 173
18:31-33 20
24:25-27 61
24:44-48 99
24:44-46 61
24:45 14
24:46-49 63
24:46-48 14
24:49 15, 85, 99

John
1:11 43
1:14 56
1:36 92
1:37 92
1:43-45 57
3:8 127
3:34 119
5:28-29 65
5:39 57
5:45-46 57
6:5-7 21
6:39-40 65
6:44-45 43
13:33 19
14:1-3 65
14:2 20
14:3 20
14:4-6 20
14:6 51, 72
14:12 20, 27, 135, 136
14:13 136
14:16-17 33
14:16 108, 153
14:17 51
14:26 45, 51, 54, 153, 154
15:5 29
15:7 137

John, cont.,
15:16 138
15:26 33, 45, 51, 153, 154
16:5-8 24
16:7-11 136
16:7-8 153
16:8 154
16:12-15 45
16:13-15 51
16:13-14 153
16:13 33, 54, 153, 154
16:14a 50
17:17 47

Acts
1:4-5 100
1:8-9 74, 100, 106
1:15 22
2:2-4 107
2:3f 157
2:4 108
2:6 107
2:8 107
2:11 107
2:14-17 24
2:16-17 107
2:29-33 25
2:41 25
3:1-8 107
3:18 58
4:4 25
4:7 108
4:8 108
4:12 72
4:13 125, 170
4:13ff. 125
4:29 125, 170
4:30 125
4:31 108, 125, 170
5:3 154
5:14 25
5:42 74

6:1 25
6:2-4 87
6:3 114
6:4 136, 140
6:5 114
6:7 25
7:51 154
7:55 114
8:5 74
8:29 154
8:35 74
9:15 109
9:17-18 28
9:17 108
9:20 74, 109
9:31 25
9:35 25
9:40 22
9:42 26
10:19-23 154
10:33 158
10:42 85
10:43 58
11:20 74
11:21 26
11:24 26, 114
12:24 26
13:2 154
13:8-11 109
13:32 85
13:48-49 26
13:52 114
14:1 26
14:12 90
16:5 26
16:14 14
17–18 70
17:2-3 58, 74
17:4 26
17:11-12 26
17:18 70
17:34 70
18:5 75

18:8 26
18:11 75
18:25 157
19:20 26
20:28 154
22:14-15 109
26:22-23 58
28:23 58
28:31 78

Romans
1:1-3 56
1:7 85
1:15 85
8:7 41
8:9 108
8:26-27 154
8:39 153
9:32 130
10:13-14 85
10:14-17 122
12:3ff 162
12:11 157
15:30 155
16:25-27 56

1 Corinthians
1:17-18 77
1:17 74, 83, 95, 101, 120
1:18-25 68
1:18 69, 70, 72, 77
1:21 69, 83
1:23 69, 70, 74, 77, 83, 89, 130
1:26-31 68
1:26-28 121
2:1-5 67, 68
2:1-2 77
2:1 69, 83, 95, 101, 120
2:2 70
2:3 92
2:3-5 143
2:4-5 100, 120, 128

1 Corinthians cont.,
2:4 84, 90, 95, 101,
  102, 109, 120
2:6 101
2:11 154
2:14 42
3:5 147
4:1 70
7:29 67
9:16 85
12–14 162
12:11 154
14:40 157
15:11 85

2 Corinthians
2:16 130, 146
4:4 13
4:5 74, 92
4:7 143, 144
4:8-10 144
5:11 90, 101
12:7-10 144

Galatians
3:1 74
5:16-24 108

Ephesians
1:15-19 44
2:1 13, 51
3:8 74
3:14-21 167
4:3 155
4:11ff. 162

4:17-18 13
4:17-18 41
4:29-30 154
6:10-20 162
6:12 168
6:14-17 168
6:16 157
6:17 142
6:18-20 168
6:18-19a 169
6:19b-20 169
6:19 125

Colossians
1:28-29 110
2:4 90
4:2-4 167

1 Thessalonians
1:2-5 124
1:5 110
1:6 125
1:9 125
2:13 125
5:19 156
5:20-22 157

2 Thessalonians
3:1 167

1 Timothy
5:17 87
6:11 141, 147

2 Timothy
1:14 70
1:6 157
2:15 142
3:14-17 140
3:14-15 55
3:16 35, 55, 141
3:17 147
4:2 85

Titus
1:15 41

Hebrews
4:12 38
10:29 154
12:7-10 153

James
1:21 158

1 Peter
1:10-12 55
1:12 110
1:23 38
2:2 158
2:8 130
3:15-16 122

2 Peter
1:20-21 35

Revelation
3:20 133
7:9 23

PERSONS INDEX

Adams, Jay 79, 152, 161
Barrett, C. K., 78, 90
Barth, Karl 29, 66, 71, 78, 80
Baxter, Richard 13, 148
Beeke, Joel 177
Begg, Alastair 130
Bernard, J. H. 65
Best, Ernest 157
Bloesch, Donald 29, 64, 122, 162
Bonhoeffer, Dietrich 94, 149
Bounds, E. M., 129
Bridges, Charles 47, 72, 78, 80, 138, 147
Brown, Charles 163
Brown, Colin 95
Bruce, F. F., 114
Bruce, Robert 149
Bunyan, John 130
Calvin, John 38, 46, 48, 53, 64, 97, 103
Carson, D. A., 28, 45, 65, 89, 95, 96, 136, 147
Chapell, Bryan 64, 65, 78, 79
Clowney, Edmund 59, 62, 64, 65
Coggan, Donald 71
Conzelmann, Hans 95
Dallimore, Arnold 113
Dodd, C. H., 71, 78
Fee, Gordon 95
Fish, Henry 129, 147
Flavel, John 66, 91, 116
Fleming, Robert 149
Frame, James E. 162
Gardiner, George 64
Green, Michael 17
Greidanus, Sidney 64, 78, 84
Henry, Matthew 36, 45
Hervey, James 98
Hildebrandt, Wilf 114
Hodge, Charles 123, 155, 168
James, John Angel 131, 177
Jennings, John 65
Jeremias, Joachim 147
Johnson, Robert 93
Jones, Thomas F. 78
Kelly, Douglas 147
Kistemaker, Simon 129
Knox , John 149
Lightfoot, J. B. 163
Lloyd-Jones, Martyn 7, 8, 16, 32, 46, 88, 94, 95, 96, 100, 103, 110, 113, 114, 126, 165

Luther, Martin 103
Manton, Thomas 29
Marcel, Pierre 42, 44, 47, 48, 87, 95, 130, 152, 171
McCheyne, Robert M., 93
Miller, Calvin 97, 127, 131, 147
Morris, Leon 28
Mueller, J. Theodore 65
Murray, Iain H., 16, 46, 148, 177
Murray, John 17
Niebuhr, R. Gustav 93
Ortland, Ray 163
Owen, John 38, 42, 46, 47, 65
Packer, J. I., 13, 34, 45, 50, 64, 79, 149, 160
Parker, Joseph 148
Payson, Edward 115, 139, 147
Peterson, Eugene 158
Piper, John 91, 92
Ramm, Bernard 45, 48, 56, 65, 130
Reynolds, Bishop 66, 79
Robertson, A. T., 90, 129
Sanders, Oswald 92
Sargent, Tony 93, 103, 114
Sibbes, Richard 39, 46
Smith, Thomas 78
Spring, Gardiner 148, 164, 172
Spurgeon, C. H., 14, 16, 17, 53, 64, 65, 97, 103, 112, 116, 126, 130, 145, 148, 149, 151, 156, 159, 161, 165
Still, William 35, 45, 65, 116, 148
Stott. John 89, 95, 96, 112, 130, 148, 155
Tasker, R. G. V. 64
Taylor, Hudson 145
Thomas, Geoffrey 16, 131, 147,
Thomas, Robert L. 157, 162
Thornwell, James Henley 140
Turner, Nigel 129
Tyerman, Luke 113
Vinet, A. 141
Warfield, B. B. 114
Watson, Thomas 80
Wells, James 148
Wesley, Charles 98
Wesley, John 97, 98, 113
Whitefield, George 97, 98, 99, 103
Williams of Pantycelyn 164
Winslow, Octavius 36, 45
Worley, R. C. 78

SELECTED THEMES

Danger of intellectualism 11ff.
Church Growth techniques 30-31
Greater Works 17-28, 32
Holy Spirit
    applies Bible to preacher 38
    empowering 14
    fire that can be quenched 156ff.
    glorifies Jesus Christ 48ff.
    grieved by congregation's wrong responses to the word 152ff.
    illumination 40ff.
    makes preaching effective 124ff.
    promised in Old Testament 24ff.
    of truth 33ff.
    sovereignty of the Spirit and human involvement 131ff.
    Spirit and Word 36ff., 54, 100ff.
Jesus Christ
    central to the gospel 73
    Holy Spirit glorifies Christ 48ff.
    revealed in Old Testament 54ff.
    as preacher 118ff.
Methodology 80ff., 100ff.
Power of God 66ff.
    revealed in the gospel 68, 70ff.
    revealed in the weakness of his servants 68, 142ff.
Powerlessness 21, 23ff., 29ff.
Prayer
    by pastors 135ff., 150ff.
    by congregation 166ff.
Preaching
    sermon preparation 37
    personal application 38
    priority of preaching 83ff.
    centrality of the gospel 72ff, 90ff., 120ff.,
    declaring not sharing 88ff.
    true effects of preaching 124ff.
Psychology 30
Scriptures
    Christ centered 52ff,
    divine revelation 34ff.
    importance of diligent study of scriptures 140ff.
    Old Testament reveals Christ 54ff.
    Word and Spirit 36ff., 54, 100ff.,